*Cardinal Memories*

# Cardinal Memories

## Recollections from Baseball's Greatest Fans

### EDITED BY TINA WRIGHT

*University of Missouri Press*

COLUMBIA AND LONDON

University of Missouri Press, Columbia, Missouri 65201
Printed and bound in Thailand

5  4  3  2  1    04  03  02  01  00

Library of Congress Cataloging-in-Publication Data

Cardinal memories : recollections from baseball's greatest fans / Tina Wright, editor.
    p.   cm.
    ISBN 1-2689 -(pb-k. : alk. paper)
    1. St. Louis Cardinals (baseball team) —History.
    2. Baseball fans—United States. I. Wright, Tina
1965–

GV875.S3 C35 2000
796.357'64'0977866—dc21

                                                    99-053656

This paper meets the requirements of the
American National Standard for Permanence of Paper
for Printed Library Materials, Z39.48, 1984.

Text design: Elizabeth K. Young
Cover design: Vickie Kersey DuBois
Typesetter: Crane Composition, Inc.
Printer and binder: International Printing Services (IPS)
Typefaces: Pepita, Century Expanded

For St. Louis Cardinal fans everywhere

# Contents

# Acknowledgments

This book would not have been possible without a lot of help and team effort. Many thanks to Henry Hager, Jonathan Pitts and Steve Weinberg for their advice and guidance in the early stages of the project; to John Vuch, for his invaluable assistance and encouragement; to Lisa Shively, a most generous and understanding employer and friend; and to Donnie Thompson—Donnie, you were my rock and we both know it. Thanks also to Bob and Randy Costas, Michael Gomez, Floid Wright, Ben Sandmel, Tracy King, Anita Mandell, Kim Webber and John Zarling. I'm indebted to Beverly Jarrett and everyone at the University of Missouri Press, who saw this book's potential, and whose enthusiasm and integrity made its publication a joyful process. Thank you also to all in the St. Louis news media who helped spread the word about the story search, specifically Bernie Miklasz and the *St. Louis Post-Dispatch,* Randi Naughton and KTVI/Fox 2, Randy Karraker and Ron Jacober at KMOX, and Rich Gould and Bob Ramsey at KFNS. Special thanks to Jack Gilbert and Bing Devine for their many kindnesses—they are gentlemen in every sense of the word; and to this book's contributors, who took the time to share their heartfelt recollections: This book belongs to all of us. Much gratitude and love go to Mike Shannon, Jack Buck and Joe Buck, and the St. Louis Cardinals, past and present. Finally, to Helen Wright, thanks Mom, for being this book's first ear, and my guiding light. This project has truly been blessed.

# Cardinal Memories

*Enos "Country" Slaughter at Fairgrounds Park in St. Louis, 1937.* (Photograph courtesy of Hortense Zingsheim)

# *Introduction* TALES FROM THE GRANDSTAND

**Tina Wright**

I stumbled into Cardinal baseball at a serendipitous moment—April 1981—when the team was poised for a decade of greatness. I was 16 years old that spring, and went to spend the weekend with my grandmother, who lived in the country. The spindly antenna perched on her roof captured only one channel clearly, KSDK Channel 5, and that weekend Channel 5 televised three Cardinal games. After I exhausted my supply of reading material, and lamented the absence of cable, or at least another network or two, I succumbed to the "if you can't beat 'em, join 'em" mentality, and sat down next to my grandma to watch the game. At that moment, Mike Ramsey dove for a ball, leaped up and started a double play to end the inning. The Cards came to bat. Tommy Herr got a hit and promptly stole second. It was fast-paced, exciting, and I was hooked.

I'd never before watched baseball, but by Sunday I was an impassioned (dare I say obsessed?) fan. I'd learned the rudiments of the game and most of the Cardinals' roster, and from that day on I followed every pitch. It seemed a cruel irony when the strike began only months after I'd discovered the Redbirds. Once-glorious summer days now stretched interminably; I could no longer remember what I had done before baseball. To this day, I can't hear the name of then-Commissioner Bowie Kuhn without thinking of that "split-season," and how the Cardinals, who finished 1981 with the NL East's best overall record, were robbed. But I guess 1982 made up for that.

Five years ago I relocated from Missouri to Nashville, Tennessee. Nashville, while rich in culture and history, and steeped in the traditions of the Old South, lacks one thing: It is not a baseball town. St. Louis is synonymous with the Cardinals; when in Missouri, I'd never wanted for the smallest detail on the team. But suddenly I found myself displaced from other fans, devoid of anything more than a box score, and straining my ears to pick up KMOX's static-filled late-night broadcasts.

Fortunately, a couple years back I signed on to America Online and discovered a St. Louis Cardinal message board. Here at last was a place to keep abreast of the Cardinals' activities, and to discuss every facet of the organization and team. A core group of us regularly exchanged views, and eventually talk turned to Cardinal teams past. One by one, we shared stories of how we became St. Louis fans. Reading those stories, I realized that, for diehard followers, the Cardinals are a part of our lives in a way that transcends hobby. Those posts were the genesis of this book: a history of the team as seen through the eyes and hearts of its fans.

Interwoven with the passion we feel for the Redbirds is an immense sense of pride in their accomplishments. There are only a handful of storied franchises in baseball; few teams can boast the equivalent of the

Cardinals' 19th-century origins, countless individual achievement records, 15 National League pennants and nine World Series titles, and cast of on-field characters that St. Louis has been fortunate enough to see. We've had more than our share of baseball's greatest moments. My sensibilities were formed by Whitey Herzog's 1980s teams, teams built for turf and predicated on speed and defense, and many of my most indelible memories are of "Whiteyball." There was the home opener in 1982, when the Cards played like April fools, and Steve Mura got bombed. I didn't care. It was the first game I, as a new fan, attended. My favorite Cardinal in those days was the self-proclaimed "One Tough Dominican," Joaquin Andujar. He was a showman with outlandish flair, occasionally raising opponents' ire by pretending to shoot them after they struck out. He was frequently the butt of clubhouse jokes, which he suffered with good humor. He was cocky, but not afraid to laugh at himself, and he could flat-out pitch. Some of my most cherished memories are of watching him on the mound.

I was also a big supporter of Keith Hernandez and, aside from the travesty of 1985, the saddest day for me as a fan was when we sent Hernandez to New York for Neil Allen. I cried when I heard the news. The next morning, I went into a florist's shop. The lady ahead of me was purchasing a lush, mixed bouquet, which had been spray-painted black. I remarked about the flowers, and she told me they were meant as a humorous gift for a disconsolate Hernandez fan.

The St. Louis Cardinals are also responsible for introducing me to one of the best friends I've ever had,

Mike Shannon. I've never met him, but oh the many pleasurable, tense, exciting and frustrating hours we've shared. Whether he's extolling the merits of a "cold, frosty Busch" or pronouncing that "ol' Abner's done it again," Mike's voice has never failed to offer reassurance, induce a smile and make me feel like I'm right there with him in the next seat. Much like Harry Caray was, Mike is one part broadcaster, two parts fan. I like knowing he is as excited about the Cardinals as I am.

Cardinal baseball has been an integral part of my life since that long-ago weekend at my grandma's. I've been witness to two truly great moments in St. Louis history: the four home games of the 1982 World Series, and Mark McGwire's 60th home run in 1998. But I treasure equally the thousands of other games I've followed when I was not at Busch Stadium, some of them pivotal victories in a championship year, others merely part of a season past. I remember autumn afternoons glued to the television, and falling asleep curled up next to the radio, listening to KMOX; I remember games I've watched in other cities, while sparring with rowdy opposition fans, and the games I've followed "online," with the play-by-play transcribed to me by a friend. Baseball is best shared. This game, this team, has enriched my life immeasurably. And I am not alone.

Many writers have tried to break down baseball's unique appeal, to analyze why it has remained *the* defining American sport, and a constant throughout centuries. We know that, quite simply, baseball is an American game. Its singular genius may be that its old heroes live on. One cannot appreciate Mark

McGwire's 70 home runs without the context of Ruth and Maris. Indeed, they were as much a part of the historic 1998 season as Mac and Sammy Sosa.

It's also been said that baseball has been a metaphor for this country's evolution; it has mirrored our popular culture, the chasms between labor and management, our race relations. And it often has been noted that the game offers a pastoral escapism from the rigors of daily life, and continuity in the midst of change. It is a means of binding generations of families—through shared experiences playing, watching or collecting. Baseball allows us to be part of something bigger than ourselves. Whether we are in the stands, or at home with the radio or TV, we are not individuals when we follow the Cardinals; we are a collective one.

I believe all of those things are true. But, it may be that what ultimately makes baseball so appealing is something very simple: The game is about hope. I know some fellow Cardinal fans who believe themselves to be pessimists, but they are not. Following baseball is a decidedly optimistic pastime. It's about might be's, could be's and percentages. It's about looking ahead to the future. No matter the Cardinals' record, or if the bats are slumping, or there is a bit of shakiness in the bullpen—we who follow the game know that the next at-bat, the next series or the next season could lead to victory, and greatness. This game—and for Cardinal fans, this team—holds our dreams, and limitless possibilities.

## Tom Heidger  ARNOLD, MISSOURI

In the summer of 1964, when I was seven, the Cardinals traded for Lou Brock. Overnight, Lou became a great offensive player and an instant hero in St. Louis. I believe he batted over .400 in the '64 World Series, which the Cards won. Back then, in my neighborhood, summer meant baseball: watching it, reading about it, playing it, or playing a variation such as Indian ball, Whiffle ball, hot box, or my personal favorite, "three grounders or a fly." But the single most important thing in life was my baseball card collection—Topps, which were packaged five cards and a piece of that inimitable gum, at a nickel a pack. In the summer of '65, my fellow collectors and I breathlessly awaited the Lou Brock card, as this would be the first time Brock was pictured as a Cardinal, not a Cub.

A few months went by, and the first six checklists, and still the Brock card had not come out. My friend Steve and I were exasperated at this situation. We would wonder aloud what pose Lou was striking in the photo. Bat on shoulder? Follow-through shot? Kneeling as if on deck? Or maybe a glove pose, as if about to catch a fly ball.

Sometime in early August, Steve discovered that Paul's Market at I-70 and Bermuda Road not only sold baseball cards but had the seventh checklist. The seventh checklist! In his quest to be the first guy to have

Lou Brock, Steve kept this knowledge to himself, something about which I would later be highly indignant. One afternoon, here came old Steve on his bike down Atherstone Drive, arms in the air, in a state of utter jubilation and triumph, hollering to the heavens at the top of his lungs: "I got Brock! I got Brock!" His bike veered to the curb and Steve took a tumble, resulting in bloodied elbows and knees. My friend was unfazed by his wounds, and had cradled the coveted card against his stomach so that it not be defaced in any way. I rushed to Steve's side, not to offer concern for his condition, but to set eyes on THE CARD. And there was Louis Clark Brock, in a Cardinal uniform, bat over left shoulder. Steve would not allow me to handle THE CARD, but in an uncharacteristic gesture of generosity, he offered me a piece of Topps gum, "compliments of the house."

# *Jeffrey Fister* ST. LOUIS

I pulled into the gas station near my house around 7:30 P.M. I had the radio tuned to the baseball game and I paid attention as the Cardinals put the first two batters on in the fifth inning. I hopped out of the van, but left the radio on loud enough to hear as I started pumping gas.

Nearby, I heard the thumpa-thumpa of loud rap music as an old truck rumbled to a stop at an adjacent gas pump. Annoyed, I turned the radio up louder. Ray Lankford was the third batter in the inning. He walked on four pitches. Now the bases were loaded and nobody was out. Next up . . . Mark McGwire.

As I strained to hear, the rap music suddenly stopped. A second later, the truck had also tuned in the ball game. On a hot, steamy summer night in St. Louis, I wondered how many people stopped what they were doing to see, or hear, what McGwire would do.

He struck out.

I looked over at the "rap" truck and a young man looked at me. He threw up his hands and laughed. "Maybe next time," he yelled.

When writers or movie-makers get sentimental about baseball, I usually don't like it. I never sat through Ken Burns' nine-hour PBS documentary and I couldn't finish Roger Kahn's *The Boys of Summer.* I

*Jeff Fister and son James dressed and ready for Cardinal action.* (Photograph courtesy of Jeff Fister)

did like *Field of Dreams*, but thought the father-son plot was too syrupy. However, like it or not, I realize that I have marked key events of my own life with baseball.

Growing up in St. Louis, I was one of those transistor-radio-under-the-pillow kids who would stay up late listening to the Cardinals play the West Coast teams. For my fifth birthday my dad, who knew the late broadcaster Harry Caray, brought me up to the broadcast booth in old Sportsman's Park and Caray gave me an autographed baseball.

In fourth grade, I got out of school one day when the Cards were playing the Detroit Tigers in the World Series. We lost 13–1, but I'll always remember the red, white and blue bunting that circled the field.

In junior high school, I would take the Redbird Express bus line with a friend downtown from Westroads Shopping Center in Richmond Heights to watch the teams of the early '70s. That was back when one misguided promotion was "Bat Night" and they actually gave the bats out *before* the game. Imagine a stadium full of adolescents with real baseball bats.

In 1982, I watched with my future wife in a bar on Laclede's Landing the final game of the World Series when we beat the Brewers. When the game ended, we raced into the streets to join the people coming out of the stadium in a wild celebration.

And when we bought our home in 1992, I thought it was a good omen that as we toured the house, its occupants had a radio tuned to the ball game in every room, and baseball memorabilia lined all of the walls.

These days my relationship with baseball is primarily through the radio. I only attend a few games each year. With grown-up responsibilities and busy schedules, I sometimes find it almost a chore to go. But the beauty of radio is you can take the game with you. Like cicadas, Jack Buck is part of the background music of summer.

In 1998, when Mark McGwire was chasing history, I went to a game with my 13-year-old son. While it wasn't a *Field of Dreams* moment, it was fun. My son got caught up in the game, even though Big Mac didn't hit a home run and we lost. Afterwards, we watched for the ballplayers to come out of their parking lot. Several hundred people waited patiently for a chance to get an autograph as luxury sport utility vehicles sped by. Would McGwire make an appearance? Time dragged on and finally Brian Jordan came out and cheerfully signed everything thrust at him. We waited a while longer for Mac, but he never showed. Maybe next time.

# Henry J. Schvey ST. LOUIS

I t was a typical cold and drizzly October evening in the Netherlands. My wife and I had received the rare honor of being invited to dine at the U.S. Ambassador's home in The Hague. Despite the luxury surrounding me, and the magnificent cuisine brought in by waiters in black tie on bone china plates encircled with slender bands of gold, I could think of only one thing that memorable evening of October 19, 1982—the St. Louis Cardinals and the impossible task facing them that day.

It was Game Six of the World Series, and the Cardinals trailed the Milwaukee Brewers three games to two. Worse, in the sixth and probably final game of the Series, a raw rookie with the unprepossessing name of Stuper was set to face the Brewers' best pitcher and future Hall-of-Famer, Don Sutton. When the lavish but interminable evening finally ended, we raced home and I sat in our kitchen with a Heineken and tried to get the game on the Armed Forces Network. Unfortunately, the reception, always unpredictable at best, was terrible. In helpless fury at not knowing the Cardinals' fate, I telephoned the U.S. Embassy. No answer. After perhaps 20 rings of agony, a Marine answered the phone. "Excuse me, would you happen to know who won the game today?" I asked with anticipated relief.

"What game, sir?" was his stern reply.

"The World Series game between the Brewers and the—"

"I don't like baseball, sir. My game's football. Auburn Tiger football."

"Yes, I understand, but surely someone there at the embassy . . . ?"

"Nope," he said, and hung up.

I started to grow desperate, and felt angry that our country could have a Marine on duty who was so indifferent to our national pastime. Then I remembered my in-laws, back in the U.S. Surely they would know who won? Why not call them right now? But my frustration only increased as, in those days without answering machines, the phone again rang remorselessly. I yelled and punched my defective (but otherwise innocent) radio as hard as I could.

What I did next was so strange and out of character that only a pure baseball addict could possibly comprehend: I began randomly dialing telephone numbers with the St. Louis area code of 314. It took, unbelievably, several calls before I was fortunate enough to find someone at home. "Hello, you don't know me. Hello! I am calling from the Netherlands and I can't find out who won today's Series game . . . I know it's late, ma'am, but if it's that late there in St. Louis, think how late it is here in Europe . . . Yes, get your husband." When the kind gentleman told me the score had been 13–1, I refused to believe him. "And

Stuper went all the way? Are you sure? With a three-hour rain delay? Really? Hernandez and Porter both homered? Thank you, sir. Goodnight."

Finally, my odyssey was complete. And, after cleaning up what was left of the Magnavox, I went to bed.

# *Mike Lanning*    WICHITA, KANSAS

I've been a Cardinal fan since the '50s. The highlight was the radio broadcast of the game-winning play against the Cubs on August 14, 1967. I was sitting in the kitchen at home in Valley Center, Kansas, listening to KMOX. Thank goodness I was getting pretty good reception that night.

The Cardinals had entered the bottom of the ninth down 5-3. They scored one and had Brock and Flood on base with Maris at bat. Harry Caray had been saying that he had a feeling the Cardinals would come back and win. He was probably as excited throughout the game as I can ever recall. How I remember the next moments as Harry shouted, "The pitch to Maris—here it is—BASE HIT! THE GAME IS TIED! HERE GOES FLOOD AROUND SECOND AS SAVAGE FUMBLES THE BALL! HERE'S FLOOD—HE'S GOING TO TRY TO SCORE! THE THROW—SAFE! CARDS WIN! CARDS WIN! CARDS WIN! HOLY COW! CARDS WIN! ROGER MARIS DID IT! SAVAGE FUMBLED THE BALL! FLOOD KEPT RUNNING AND BEAT THE THROW TO THE PLATE! I TOLD YOU I—I HAD A FEELING WE WERE GOING TO WIN THIS GAME!"

It was about this time I realized that I hadn't taken

a breath since Maris hit the ball. I think I was about ready to pass out. Thanks Harry. And since then, thanks Jack and Mike. Radio is still the best way to "see" a ball game if you can't be there. People like Harry and Jack make it that way.

*Raymond Warfel*  HONG KONG

## "Vinegar Bend and Smitty"

I'm 55 years old and have a great Cardinal story from my childhood that I will never forget. When I tell people about it they find it hard to believe. The years were 1956–1958 and the Cardinal players involved were batterymates: left-handed pitcher Wilmer "Vinegar Bend" Mizell and catcher Hal Smith. Both were Christian men who regularly attended services with their families at the Florissant Valley Baptist Church. They always attended the early service, which allowed them time to get to the old ballpark (Sportsman's Park at Grand and Dodier) for the usual Sunday doubleheader.

As teenagers and devoted Cardinal fans, my buddies and I would mow lawns during the week (can you believe we got a dollar per lawn, sometimes with a 25 cent tip?) to scrape together three or four dollars, enough to go see our beloved Cardinals play. To get the most value for our hard-earned money, we always went to Sunday doubleheader games, arrived early to see all the pre-game batting practice (long before the current McGwire phenomenon) and hung around outside the players' exit from the locker rooms after the games to collect autographs. We usually got in a 10- to 12-hour day of baseball on Sundays and the only drawback was our unreliable transportation to and from Florissant. We depended on a combination of hitchhiking, buses and streetcars, including transfers at Ferguson and Wellston. We frequently got strand-ed and it took forever to get home, sometimes after midnight.

The players were remarkably friendly and generous to the fans in those days. They always devoted time to signing autographs and the visiting team would chat with fans through the windows of their chartered bus. The hometown Cardinals drove to the park and usually carpooled, which Mizell and Smith always did, sometimes with other players who lived in Florissant, like Wally Moon.

We had autographs from everyone from superstars (Musial, Mays, Koufax, Banks and Aaron) to umpires and even batboys and clubhouse assistants (Doggie Lynch). No player ever refused to sign, at least for a few minutes, and no one ever considered the crazy notion of charging the fans money for an autograph.

After one particularly long Sunday that included an extra-inning game, one of my buddies was scared we would be so late getting home that his parents would punish him. He kept begging us to leave before the game ended but the rest of us wouldn't hear of it. Besides wanting to see the game itself, we had invested 75 cents each in bleacher tickets, crawled behind the shrubs in center field to get into the 90-cent pavilion seats in right field, and scaled a 15-foot fence in full public view to get into the general admission section. By the second game we had worked our way

*Former St. Louis Cardinal catcher Hal Smith, left, poses with Ray Warfel at Smith's home in Texas.* (Photograph courtesy of Ray Warfel)

into empty box seats right behind the "on deck" circle, as close to heaven as any of us could imagine. No way were we going to leave before the last out of the game and the autograph ritual. No item on our precious Sunday agenda of baseball was to be sacrificed.

After the game we made our way to the players' exit. Soon Mizell and Smith appeared. In panicked desperation to get home, our frightened friend had the nerve, audacity, or whatever to mention to them that we also lived in Florissant, attended the same church they did, and *could we please have a ride home with them?* To our amazement, they said, "Sure." The next thing we knew we were sitting in the back seat of their car discussing the day's games. Wally Moon was also in the car and he mentioned playing shortstop in the minor leagues. I knew Moon batted left-handed and I asked him how a lefty could play shortstop. He clarified that while he batted left, he threw right-handed. I was mortified not to know this and my friends were silently kicking and poking me to make me shut up and stop embarrassing them with my ignorance about our local hero.

The players insisted on driving out of their way, safely delivering us to our homes instead of dropping us at the nearest major street. Our families and neighbors recognized the players as they dropped us off and waved goodnight. This soon became a regular routine, with Smith and Mizell recognizing us at church on Sunday mornings and looking for us as they left the clubhouse to return home on Sunday nights. They got to know our names and even talked to us about our Little League baseball teams.

I am determined someday to write to these two wonderful men or their families and tell them that their humanity and kindness to children some 40-plus years ago is still remembered, cherished and never to be forgotten.

One footnote: Harry Caray nicknamed Mizell "Vinegar Bend" after Wilmer's hometown in Alabama.

Harry always claimed it was his favorite baseball player hometown. Of course, Harry had about 500 "favorite" hometowns of players. Another was Strawberry Plains, the hometown of Ed Bailey, former catcher for the Cincinnati Reds.

[Editor's note: Wilmer Mizell passed away on February 21, 1999, at the age of 68. A few months earlier, Mr. Warfel spoke via phone with "Vinegar Bend," and relayed some of the highlights of that conversation: Mizell, who served as a congressman from his home state of North Carolina from 1968 to 1974, had remained active in congressional baseball games, serving as a bench coach. When asked if he could still teach the high leg kick that was his trademark as a pitcher (Willie Mays loved it because he didn't even have to slide when stealing second base), Wilmer laughed and replied, "That's about all that's left." He still remembered giving rides home to some kids more than 40 years ago.

Ray also spoke with Hal Smith and subsequently visited him at Hal's home in Texas. Smitty recently retired from scouting for the Cardinals. He related that the autograph requests he now receives by mail are usually accompanied by a check for $5 or $10. He always returns both his autograph and the uncashed check, believing to this day that fans should not have to pay for autographs. He and Mizell remained good friends.]

# *Dalton Sullivan*   ST. LOUIS

I t is impossible to say exactly when I became an adult and no longer a child. There was no magical moment, no date when the baton was passed from adolescence to manhood. I didn't wake up one morning, and suddenly look at the world with a whole new perspective. But I can say, with all certainty, that the summer of 1964 forever changed me. That was when baseball became an everyday part of my life.

That summer, I turned seven years old, and several important things happened. First, I played Little League for the first time. Where? At the ABC fields in St. Ann. My first team? The Flyers. I played shortstop, because my favorite player was Dick Groat. Second, I somehow talked my mom and dad into subscribing to *Sports Illustrated* for me. My first issue featured Jim Bunning and Chris Short of the Philadelphia Phillies on the front. They were smiling first-place smiles. Later that summer, the smiles would fade. Finally, sometime in June or July, my grandfather had the wisdom and foresight to buy four tickets, one for himself, one for my dad, and one each for my brother and me, to the last game of the regular season: October 4, 1964.

Even though I was only seven, I paid close attention to the pennant race. I listened to KMOX, from which Harry Caray and Jack Buck came into my room every night. I had a pocket-sized transistor radio that I would hold under the covers to listen to the games. I knew the Phillies had a seemingly insurmountable lead as we headed into September, but I also knew that I was going to my first baseball game in just a matter of weeks, with the two men who had instructed me, coached me, and taught me a love and respect for the game that grew stronger every day.

As the day drew closer, something strange was happening. The Phillies couldn't win, and the Cardinals couldn't lose. A 10-game Philadelphia lead vanished in two weeks. As the final weekend arrived, the Cardinals, Phillies and Reds were all within one game of each other. The Phils and Reds were playing each other, while the Cardinals hosted the lowly New York Mets. The final day, Sunday the fourth, saw the Cards one game ahead of the Phillies, and tied with the Reds. If the Cardinals lost for a third straight time to the Mets, and the Phillies beat the Reds, then baseball would have its first-ever three-way tie.

As we walked from our car to Sportsman's Park, I couldn't help but notice that the street we were on was Sullivan Avenue. "Yes," I thought, "This is going to be a good day." As we entered, the cathedral of green spread out before us like an ever-widening horizon. The grass was a deep emerald, the uniforms whiter than white, the red hats stunning in their hue. I know, I was only seven years old, but I was finally at the place where the people I'd listened to, the players I'd imitated, the sights I had imagined, were all laid out before me. There was my favorite player, Dick Groat. There were others who became famous after they left St. Louis, as well: Tim McCarver, Bob Uecker, Bill White. The veterans: Kenny Boyer, Curt Flood, Bob Gibson, Lou Brock, Bob Skinner, Curt Simmons, Roger Craig, Ray Sadecki. The local boys: Mike Shannon, Jerry Buchek, Dal Maxvill. The role players: Charlie James, Carl Warwick, Ron Taylor, Gordon Richardson, Mike Cuellar, Barney Schultz, Ray Washburn. Their faces, their images, their numbers are as fresh today as they were that sunny fall afternoon years ago.

The story of what happened that day is well documented. The Cardinals beat the Mets, the Phillies beat the Reds, and St. Louis won its first pennant in 18 years. One of my memories of that day, after Barney Schultz retired the side in the ninth, is of the fans jumping, leaping and falling out of the outfield stands. My brother and I both wanted to go out on the field as well. I'm sure it was all my grandpa and dad could do to keep the two of us from running out there.

On the wall of my home I have a picture. It is a photograph of the 1964 World Champion St. Louis Cardinals. Beside the picture are four ticket stubs, all bearing the date "October 4, 1964." The section is X, row 17, seats 18, 19, 20 and 21. The cost of each ticket was $2.25. The memory of each ticket is priceless.

# T. J. Crawford

RALEIGH, NORTH CAROLINA

Tommy Herr was like a god to me when I was growing up. He wasn't the most prolific player on the team, but he had the heart to make things happen. While other kids were crazy over Ozzie and his back-flips, I loved to watch Tommy bat, or complete a double play. One game in particular, against the Cubs, sticks out in my mind. Harry Caray was the broadcaster (on WGN), and Tommy was up to bat. Harry said that Tommy had fewer than 10 home runs in the previous year, and questioned why he was batting third in the Cards' lineup. He also commented that the outfielders needed to move in. At that moment Tommy pounded a home run. Harry didn't say a single bad word about Tommy for the rest of the game.

I also remember the 1985 World Series when Tommy was robbed on a play at first. I had never seen Tommy get angry before, so I was really mad at Kansas City, and umpires, after that. Whenever I played in a Little League game, I would give the umps a suspicious look. I got to meet Tommy back in 1985. He gave me an autograph and told me to practice throwing a rubber ball against the wall to increase agility. I broke out four windows on the side of my parents' house over the course of a month because of his advice.

When Tommy was finally traded to the Twins, I almost switched teams. I remained a Cardinal fan, but I never liked Tom Brunansky, the man who inadvertently made my hero leave St. Louis. Since Tommy, I've had other Cardinal favorites, including Bob Tewksbury and Tom Pagnozzi, but I will only have one favorite of all time, and that is the man with little power, but a big game: Tommy Herr.

# Jim Shucart    ST. LOUIS

I was born in St. Louis, and due to this happy accident, I've been fortunate to be a Cardinals fan all of my life. As a little boy, the only name I knew was "The Man," Stan Musial. When my dad came home at the end of World War II, he elected to stay in the Army, so my mom and I left St. Louis to live on a series of Army bases. I met a lot of terrific men (enlisted men in my dad's unit) who played baseball with me and looked after me. They all knew I was from St. Louis, and they nicknamed me "The Man." I secretly hoped to be like the real "Stan the Man" someday.

After my dad left the Army he went to work for Studebaker on the West Coast, and later transferred to South Bend, Indiana. When Studebaker was bought out, Dad felt the time was right to return to St. Louis. In 1954, with no job in hand, we came home. I knew nothing of this, though. All I knew was that we were going home to the land of the Cardinals. I hoped I would finally get to see my hero, for I'd never actually seen Stan play ball. I'd only heard stories, and when I was old enough to read, followed his exploits in the newspapers.

By the time we got back to St. Louis, I was 11 years old, and I'd come to accept that bad eyes meant I'd never realize my dream to be just like Stan. However, I still looked up to him as a hero and role model. He was decent, a team player, generous to his fans and the community and, by the way, about the best ballplayer in the game. Finally we got moved in and I started asking Dad when we could go to a ball game. At 11, the fact that my dad didn't have a job had no bearing on going to a ball game to see my hero play.

Each time I asked about going, Dad would say, "We'll see." Finally the day came when my dad said, "We're going next week." I was beside myself with excitement. I actually slept with my glove (a Musial model, of course) for the next six nights. I don't remember much of the trip to the park, but I recall how *big* it looked when we got there. Sportsman's Park. I remember the sights and sounds as though it were yesterday: the towering stands, the noise, the smell of popcorn, the vendors, the billboards, the flags and the huge scoreboard. "St. Louis Cardinals vs. New York Giants," it read. And not only was I going to see my first major league ball game, and my hero, but this was a doubleheader!

I don't remember much about those games except for what my hero did. Stan hit *five* home runs, and by the end of the second game, I was convinced I'd seen the greatest ballplayer who ever lived. He was more than I'd dreamed he could be. He was magnificent. To my 11-year-old eyes, he was the embodiment of everything good. I can still see the ball arching toward the right-field stands, flying high, straight and true. I can still hear the crack of the bat as he struck the ball, and see him trotting around the bases as thousands of us roared our approval. To see him hit one home run was almost more excitement than I could stand, but five home runs in one day! I was hoarse from cheering and my hands were sore from clapping, but I knew I had witnessed history. With a young boy's version of wisdom, I understood that this was something special. A hero who meets the expectations of a little boy is very rare, but on that day in 1954, Stan "The Man" Musial met and surpassed my expectations. It was magic.

On a sunny day in 1963 I was in the stadium again to see a Cardinals game—Stan's last. I remember his final at bat: the stance, a funny, coiled crouch, eyes intently staring at the pitcher; the familiar number six on his back; the crack of his bat as he drove the ball for a clean single. I remember him running to first base. I can hear the roar of the crowd as he rounded the bag, then retreated to the base as the throw from the outfield came in to second. Then a pinch runner came out to take his place, and we knew it was over. The crowd cheered. My hero walked slowly toward the dugout, pausing to tip his cap to the crowd. I was that little boy again, cheering for my idol. His gaze passed over me, and in my imagination he was thanking me for being his fan. But no thanks were needed. He would always be "The Man."

# *Ann Vitale*  ST. LOUIS

In 1980 I moved to St. Louis after a divorce. I was dating a native St. Louisan who was a great Cardinal fan. We began attending baseball games as our social event of choice and soon I, too, became filled with Cardinalmania. During the early part of the 1982 season Joe and I were still dating but I was really hoping for a marriage proposal. One evening while we were at the ballpark, Joe told me that if the Cardinals won the pennant that year we would get married. Thank goodness the team came through! Not only did they win the pennant but the World Series, too. They ensured my marriage, which was officially sealed with Cardinals in my bouquet and on Joe's lapel on June 11, 1983. We continue to be great Cardinals fans, as are our children. When we look at our wedding pictures with friends someone always asks the significance of the Cardinals in my bouquet and in Joe's lapel, and we enjoy telling the story of how the St. Louis Cardinals were instrumental in our marriage.

*Ed Kniest*   JEFFERSON CITY, MISSOURI

## "1974: The Magical Season"

Although the Cardinals did not win the pennant in 1974, that particular year remains possibly the greatest year of baseball in my life. It is most certainly my favorite.

Together with my best friend, Paul DeBernardi, I went to many games that year and was able to witness two of the greatest moments in Cardinal history: Bob Gibson's 3,000th career strikeout and Lou Brock's 105th stolen base in a single season. We went to numerous games in succession as those two Cardinal stars neared their respective marks. Paul and I wanted to be in attendance for history.

Another fond memory of that season was attending the home opener against Pittsburgh. As we usually did when we went to the ballpark, Paul and I rode the Tower Grove bus from our homes in the Compton Heights neighborhood. Since we were just 15 years old, we thought it easier to ride the bus than to pester a family member for a ride. Besides, it only cost 25 cents one-way apiece for bus fare. Combined with the $1.50 we each needed to buy a general admission ticket, it was pretty enticing to take in a game whenever we wanted.

While we were standing in line to pay our admission, an older man approached us and asked if we needed tickets. After we answered affirmatively, he said his son and daughter-in-law were unable to attend that night and since he didn't want two box seats to go to waste, we could have them for free—as long as we didn't mind sitting with him and his wife. We accepted, thanked him for his generosity, and hurried inside.

The seats were about a dozen rows up from the field along the first-base line. Imagine our surprise as we saw Stan "The Man" Musial and "Cool Papa" Bell just a few feet from us. They had thrown out the first pitches that night and were now in their seats. It took about four innings for us to work up the courage to approach them for their autographs, but we did. I treasure the scorecard they signed and I still have it safely packed away. The rest of the game remains a blur, although I recall the Redbirds won despite two home runs from Pirate third baseman Richie Hebner.

That incident led Paul and me to continue collecting autographs at other games we went to that summer. Kenny Reitz, Ted Sizemore, Bake McBride, Ted Simmons, Jose Cruz and Joe Torre were just a few of our hometown heroes who signed for us. We also got signatures from visiting players such as Chris Speier of the Giants and Manny Sanguillen of the Pirates.

However, my most special memory of the year occurred after a game on June 18. That evening, the Cardinals beat San Francisco and Lou Brock swiped a pair of bases. Brock was celebrating his 35th birthday that day and his play during the game belied the fact that he was closer to age 40 than he was to 25.

After the game, Paul and I were stationed near the players' exit, along with other autograph seekers. We had decided to head for home after about an hour or so when we noticed someone leaving from the press gate, about 30 yards away. Even though there was not much light, we quickly recognized it was Lou Brock.

We, along with a couple of other teenage stragglers, rushed toward him, shouting, "Lou! Lou! Wait up! Can we have your autograph, please?" Thankfully, he was kind enough to stop.

Lou was with his wife, and he had his hands full with gifts from his teammates. He said, "I'll be glad to sign for all of you but can we walk to my car so I can put these things in the trunk?" A chance to talk and walk along with a Cardinal great? Sure thing, Lou!

As we walked along the Seventh Street overpass to the Stadium Garage West, Lou made conversation with the four or five of us who followed in his wake. Did we like the game? Where did we go to school?

About then, Paul noticed the roar of the last Tower Grove bus pulling out from the bus stop. "Oh, no!" he cried. "There goes the last bus." Lou asked if we were without a ride home, but I said we could call one of our moms to come pick us up. *Besides*, I thought, *I'll walk home if it means I get to talk with one of my favorite players.*

Seeing a chance to ask a question, I spoke up. "Lou," I said, "Tell the truth. You gonna break Maury Wills' record of 104 stolen bases this year?"

Lou hemmed and hawed a bit, saying, "I don't know. That's an awful lot of bases and Maury was a pretty good player."

I brushed aside such modesty and exclaimed, "C'mon, Lou. You *know* you're gonna do it. Maury's only a Dodger."

At this remark, Brock chuckled softly and smiled. "Well, maybe you're right," he said. "We'll have to see." Noting the sparkle in his eye, I knew he was seriously planning to set the mark.

By this time, we'd reached his car and, true to his word, Brock stood there and signed for us. After thanking him once again for signing, we all watched as he and his wife got into his car and drove off. The high from that encounter lasted a long time for Paul and me. In fact, it still brings a chill to me to this day when I think about it. Paul passed away three years ago but when I remember the fun and excitement of the 1974 season, it brings him alive for me once more. Thanks again, Lou, for that brief period of time almost 25 years ago, when you made the whole summer for a couple of kids from South St. Louis.

# *Terry Dickerson*  LOS ANGELES

In 1972, when I was 12 years old, my brothers and I scrounged together our lawn-cutting earnings and allowance money to take our dad to Busch Stadium for his birthday. What a day! It was *really hot* and our seats sucked, but we got to see Lou Brock make an incredible diving catch about 20 feet away from us. Hot dogs, popcorn, ice-cold sodas . . . man, I still remember it like it was yesterday. I also recall listening to the Cards on the radio on Sunday afternoons, with the smell of barbecue in the air.

My fiancée and I live in L.A., but we went back to St. Louis in 1996 for the Wizard's last three regular-season games before his retirement. We took my brother-in-law and eight-year-old nephew to the final game. The look on my nephew's face when we walked into the stadium was unbelievable! I came within about three feet of catching a foul ball for him (darn the bad luck). My fiancée grew up in California (with fair-weather Dodger and lukewarm Angel fans), and when everyone at Busch stood up and yelled "Take Me Out to the Ball Game," she turned to me and said, "Wow! You guys really love your baseball here, don't you?" Yes, we do.

# James M. Kellogg

FARMINGTON, MISSOURI

My favorite memory of the St. Louis Cardinals was attending Game One of the 1964 World Series against the famed New York Yankees. I was a senior in high school and, with or without parental permission, about a dozen of us decided to spend the night before the game waiting in line to buy standing-room-only tickets. As I recall, the "outrageous" asking price for those tickets was $3.50. This was quite an upgrade from my usual 75-cent bleacher seat.

We lined up on Dodier Street at about 9 P.M. and there was already a considerable group ahead of us. The chilly October night, and it was a long one, was spent playing touch football on the Carter Carburetor parking lot, taking restroom and warm-up breaks at the YMCA on North Grand, and making forays to the White Castle on North Florissant, while each of us in turn held our place in the line.

Anticipation mounted throughout the early daylight hours and the crowd continued to grow. About 9 A.M., word spread that the Red Cross was dispensing coffee and doughnuts on Sullivan Avenue, where the line for bleacher tickets was located. We had avoided that line the night before due to its length. The word was true and some of our scouts returned with the much-needed refreshments.

Once the gates opened and we were moving into the stadium, magic occurred. We were soon sitting under concrete abutments behind the last lower-level seats between home plate and third base, *awaiting the World Series*. The discomfort and fatigue were ignored as Mickey Mantle, Roger Maris, Yogi Berra, and the other legendary Yankees, whom none of us had ever seen play in person, took batting practice. Maris and Mantle I especially remember hitting home runs in BP, Mantle hitting one completely out of the stadium over the right-field pavilion. Fortunately, the only Yankee to hit a home run in the actual game was Tom Tresh.

The game featured Whitey Ford against Ray Sadecki, who had won 20 games for the Cardinals that year. The Cards fell behind and later tied the score on a tremendous home run by Mike Shannon off the left-field scoreboard. Curt Flood was the batting hero with a triple to drive in the winning run. The Cardinals, with help from aged knuckleballer Barney Schultz in relief, won the game.

Our Cardinals had actually beaten the infamous Yankees, and they went on to win the Series. That was the only World Series game I have ever seen and, despite the passage of 30-plus years and all of the changes that war and life experiences brought to our group, I still cherish that October day when, through bleary eyes, I saw the Cardinals triumph.

# Betty Keller Timmer

## " '67 Cardinals Made Me a Lifetime Redbird Rooter"

I don't remember much about the '64 Cardinals—just my dad, Harold, and my Uncle Eddie listening to the radio in my grandma's dining room one late September afternoon when the announcer was screaming, "The Cardinals win the pennant! The Cardinals win the pennant!" Big deal. That didn't mean much to a seven-year-old girl. Three years later, it would!

I was an only child, and my dad loved baseball. To him, there were no other sports. I remember Pop listening to the games on his "little radio" (transistor) almost every evening in the summertime. Many other people in our neighborhood did the same thing. Sitting on the front porch, we could hear the voices of Harry Caray and Jack Buck echo up and down the streets. It was hard not to become a fan.

For some reason, in 1967, I began to pay attention to those nightly broadcasts. I don't recall the exact batting order anymore, but Lou Brock played left field and was the lead-off hitter. Curt Flood followed him when a right-hander pitched, and he patrolled center field. Orlando Cepeda, my hero, was the first baseman, and Roger Maris was in right field. The rest of the everyday lineup featured Julian Javier at second, Dal Maxvill at short, Mike Shannon at third, and Tim McCarver behind the plate. The starting pitchers were Bob Gibson, Steve Carlton, Nelson Briles, Dick Hughes, and Ray Washburn, with Joe Hoerner and Ron Willis coming in for relief.

I would get so excited whenever Orlando would be on the "Dugout Show" or "Star of the Game." Harry Caray seemed to love to talk to "Cha Cha," and that's probably one reason that I liked Cepeda. Another was that Cepeda had such a wonderful season—he was the 1967 MVP. Everyone loves a star!

Our neighborhood didn't have many kids my age. We played Whiffle ball at night, with Pop being our pitcher. Even though my neighbor, Jerry, was right-handed, he would always pretend to be Lou Brock. I batted left-handed, but I would still announce, "Orlando Cepeda is at the plate."

By mid-season I was begging Pop to take me to a ball game. Busch Memorial Stadium was only a year old, and I don't think Pop had ever driven there. Going to St. Louis was a big deal for us Millstadt people, and a ball game was an even bigger deal. Finally, Pop gave in. We went to see the Cards vs. the Giants on a Sunday afternoon. We bought our general admission seats and headed out to center field, way up high. I think I was sitting in line with the flagpole, but that didn't matter; I was seeing the Cardinals. Willie Mays stole second base, but St. Louis won the game.

September brought the start of fifth grade for me, and the closing days of the baseball season. The Cardinals had pretty much locked up the National League title a long time ago, despite Bob Gibson's broken leg. The only remaining question was, "Who would they play in the World Series?" The Boston Red Sox won the pennant on the last day of the season. The World Series was ready to begin. I remember our school superintendent giving the students updates on the games over the intercom. The Cards had Bob Gibson on the mound for Game Seven, and Gibby came through again.

I've listened to a lot of Cardinal games since then, but 1967 is when my love began. Some of my fondest memories of my dad are baseball-related. Thank you, El Birdos!

*Alan Stobie*  ST. LOUIS

One day I was replacing glass for a customer, and I had to make a trip to Schnarr's True Value Hardware on Clayton Road. As I was waiting for the glass to be cut, I browsed around the store. There was a customer checking out, and I thought to myself, "That guy looks so familiar." But I couldn't place him. Then I heard the cashier call him "Stan." *Click!* "Could that be Stan Musial?" I wondered. I went out to my van, just in case, and grabbed a piece of scrap paper. As I came back in, he was leaving. I asked the cashier, "Who was that man?"

She replied, "Stan Musial." Out the door I went.

"Excuse me, Mr. Musial?" I asked. He turned around.

"Uh, sir, I know you probably get bothered for this all the time, but I thought I would ask anyway. Could I get your autograph for my son?" I held out the ratty piece of paper, along with a pen. Stan said sure, and he walked to his car and opened the trunk. He asked me what my son's name was, and I told him "Joe." He dug in his trunk and came out with a card with a picture of himself alongside his stats. He personalized it to my son, and signed it. Great! But he didn't stop there. He then dug a baseball out of his trunk, and went on to personalize it to Joe, and signed it also.

I thanked him, and as I drove away on cloud nine, I thought to myself, "If I'd known I was going to get a baseball out of this, I would have told him my son's name was Alan!"

# *Tim Graeff*  ST. LOUIS

I 'm 22 years old and was born and raised in St. Louis. Throughout my life, I have wanted nothing more than to be associated with the St. Louis Cardinals. I have so many great Cardinal memories, from Sutter and Porter hugging after the victory in '82, to watching Brian Jordan hit a home run in Game Four of the NLCS in '96 to help the Cards come back and beat the Braves. But there is one memory I'll never forget. And even though it is one of disappointment, it is a part of my Cardinal past that I will forever cherish.

In 1985 I was only nine years old, and I lived and died with the birds on the bat. My cousin and very close friend Stuart lived in Kansas City and was a huge Royals fan. We had a childish love for our teams, our cities, and most important, a love for the game. The I-70 battle was built up incredibly on the news. A rivalry was born. Just days before the Series began, my cousin and I were visiting our grandparents in southern Illinois. Our grandfather always had us help him out in the yard, raking leaves, pulling weeds, etc. After we helped him out this particular fall day he gave us each a dollar. One dollar. It was a precious thing to us to receive a whole dollar at that young age. Well, naturally, Stuart and I began talking about the

*"Best friends to this day" Tim Graeff (at right) and his cousin Stuart, prior to the 1985 World Series.* (Photograph courtesy of Tim Graeff)

upcoming Cards/Royals Series. I boasted of Ozzie Smith and Willie McGee; he bragged of Bret Saberhagen and George Brett. One thing led to another and we ended up betting our only dollars on the Series. We shook on it like little businessmen. My hope was alive with the boys in red; his was alive with K.C.

We all know what events took place over the course of that Series; I need not explain the details. The team's theme that year was Glen Frey's "The Heat is On," and even in Game Seven when things were pretty ugly for St. Louis, I still hoped the Cards would pull something off and that the "heat" would not die.

When the game ended with the final out, I was in tears. I couldn't take my eyes off of those Royals players celebrating and my Redbirds with broken hearts. But I got up, walked into my room and took the dollar out of my piggy bank. Still crying, I looked at it and stuffed it into an envelope. Writing Stuart's address on that envelope and sealing my dollar inside of it was one of the most difficult things I had ever done. No letter, just the dollar. He knew how much I loved the St. Louis Cardinals—he wouldn't need a note. I asked my mother for a stamp, and I walked out to the mailbox. All of this while the television showed champagne and smiles in the Kansas City locker room. I walked back inside, took one last look at the TV, and went to my bed. I cried myself to sleep that night.

To this day, of all of the money I've ever had pass through my hands, that one precious dollar was the most difficult debt I ever had to pay. I'll never forget it. Because to me, my Cardinals were worth my only dollar.

P.S. Denkinger still owes me a buck.

# Beverly Jaegers ST. LOUIS

## "Musial Memories"

In 1941, my family moved to the edge of St. Louis Hills, on Mardel Avenue. One of my earliest memories is walking down a sizzling-hot summertime sidewalk somewhere near that area, and listening to a Cardinals game being broadcast behind the awning-shaded screen of a small ranch home's living room window. As I was véry little at that time I have always regarded myself as a dyed-in-the-wool Cardinal fan.

Shortly after we moved to Mardel Avenue, I found that I was old enough to go down the street, barefoot, being careful not to stub my toe, and buy that most wonderful of summertime ice cream treats, a black raspberry ripple five-cent cone at Dueker's Drugs on the corner. One day I was enjoying my cone rapidly, so that it would not melt all over my hands, when I saw a large group of children buzzing around the bus stop at Watson and Mardel. Within a few moments, I discovered that they were waiting for a particular person to get off the bus. His name was Stan Musial, and he was a Cardinals ballplayer. Stan and his family lived in the second house behind Dueker's Drugs, which like most of the houses on our modern block was of red brick trimmed with white.

Joining the other children, I finished my cone and

waited with them to see the Cardinal player arrive. Shortly, the big red bus pulled up, stopped, and a tall, slender man in a gray summer suit got off. Seeing the children waiting for him, his tilted blue-gray eyes twinkled and a smile creased his tanned face. As he stepped to the concrete, we surrounded him and some of the bigger, bolder boys waved pieces of paper at Musial, asking for an "autograph." I did not know what an autograph was, so I just watched as he pulled out a pencil and cheerfully talked and grinned as he signed the papers.

After several minutes, he walked the few steps to his home, surrounded and followed by the group of laughing children, went up the sidewalk and into his house. Fascinated, my daily routine changed after that, and always included a trip to the bus stop about an hour after a day game at Sportsman's Park, to wait for Stan with the other children. We hated it and felt abandoned when the team was out of town, and would often go to the bus stop anyway, just in the hope that Stan would somehow appear.

The next year, I suffered an attack of poliomyelitis, and was not allowed to join the waiting children. I spent the whole summer inside or sitting on the porch, watching the crowd down the street and wishing I could be a part of it. In the third year, white-helmeted men patrolled our street at dusk, watching for any light that might reveal our homes as targets for enemy bombers, but the crowds continued to wait on that simmering corner in the hot afternoons. Late that summer I was allowed to begin my walks to Dueker's again, and happily joined the waiting crowd.

By then, I knew what an autograph was, but never remembered to take any paper.

It was in that same year that Dickie, Musial's son, was old enough to play with some of us and, with permission from Miss Lillian, we could go inside the fenced-in Musial yard. We soon learned that there was a plentiful supply of baseballs, gloves and bats inside the house. Looking back on this today, I wonder whether some of those balls, bats and gloves were not autographed by other baseball players and perhaps very valuable. At that time, however, we had no idea that such things might be.

We could play baseball all afternoon, even when Stan was out of town, but Dickie warned us that we had to be careful not to hit a ball over the back fence and into the witch's yard. That was a fearsome place, shaded by a huge apple tree, with tomato stakes sticking up like teeth over the fence. We were certain that if we hit a ball over there we would be eaten, at the very least. One day, alas, one of us (not me) hit a ball over the fence and into *that* yard. We scattered as if those planes were overhead ready to bomb us into oblivion. None of us knew *what* to do, and we knew that ball would never be seen again. It was a full week before the lure of Miss Lillian's Kool Aid and lemonade drew us back into the yard!

In the next summertime, when I was very old and wise (almost eight and a half), Miss Lillian one day asked me to oversee the other children while she stepped to the drugstore. My job for 20 minutes was to keep order in the Musial yard. It made me feel so grown up I almost forgot to go to the bus stop when it was time for Stan to come home. Later in the summer she asked me several times again.

It was shortly after that that a new neighbor moved in on the other side of Stan's home, and their timid daughter joined us on the corner for the first time. She became so excited when Stan stepped off the bus she jumped, and the ball of ice cream dropped off her cone onto the sidewalk. Looking down at the melting blob, she burst into tears. Seeing that, Musial looked at her for a moment, then walked grandly into the drugstore and returned with another cone for her. She was ecstatic, and he smiled a big smile as he walked down the sidewalk and home.

The very next week, I decided that it was time for me to get one of those "autographs" from Mr. Musial. I borrowed my mother's purse, put in a torn piece of homework paper, and lugged it down the street. I waved that paper and felt so big when he took it and signed it for me with a flourish. Carefully, I tucked it into the purse and walked all the way back up the street, clutching it against my blue shorts. When I got home, my little brother was playing in the yard with his friends Beano and Windy, and I put the purse down by our side door to help them pull apart a large empty box for the front of a fort.

Later, when I looked for the purse, it was gone. My mom had gone to the grocery store and taken the purse along. When she returned, I looked inside and the long-awaited autograph was gone. She had thought it was just a scrap and thrown it away. I was heartbroken, for I had lost the precious signature.

Although we lived on Mardel almost another year,

I never thought to try to get another autograph. In my mind, you only got one, and I'd lost my chance. Those wonderful years remain fresh in my mind, those summers of long ago during the war, and although I've had other chances, I still don't have Stan Musial's autograph. And Dickie Musial is probably still figuring out how to get his ball from the witch's yard!

*Jim Keith*   SULPHUR SPRINGS, MISSOURI

J ust prior to spring training in 1986 or '87, Ozzie Smith and his brother were shopping in a department store at one end of a large mall in St. Louis County. I was head of security for the store, and had stationed a couple of officers in the area, in case people approached Smith and started to bother him while he shopped. I stayed with Ozzie and his brother.

Soon, an older lady in her late 60s or early 70s recognized the Cardinal shortstop and ran up to him. "Are you *really* Ozzie Smith?" she asked. He acknowledged her with a smile and said, "Yes." She then told him that it was her grandson's birthday and he was sitting in her car in the parking lot. She asked if Ozzie would go out and tell this little boy "Happy Birthday," assuring him it would take only a couple of minutes.

Ozzie turned to his brother, handed him the various sweatsuit items he was carrying, and said he would be right back. Then he left the sporting goods department with the lady.

Ozzie returned ... about 20 minutes later. He smiled and said, "The lady was parked at the *other* end of the mall." He'd had to walk past hundreds of shoppers.

Ozzie's brother asked, "What did the kid say when you wished him Happy Birthday?"

Ozzie laughed and said, "Nothing. He just sat there in shock."

I told Smith that even though the visit took 20 minutes of his time, and the little boy was speechless, he will forever be telling his children and grandchildren about the time when he was a kid and Ozzie Smith wished him a happy birthday. I know I won't forget Ozzie's act of kindness.

# Jim Grillo    ST. LOUIS

I have been a Cardinal fan since I was a young boy and have seen many great moments in person. I was in Busch Stadium to see Bob Gibson's 3,000th strikeout, Ozzie Smith's playoff-winning home run in 1985, and Tom Lawless' homer against the Twins in 1987. My dad tells me I saw games at Sportsman's Park but all I ever did was play with the seats.

My formative baseball years were when the Cardinals had the great teams of the '60s, and I can still remember Sister Louise bringing a TV into my second-grade classroom at St. Mary Magdalen in Brentwood to watch the World Series. But my favorite memory is not something that happened on the field, but a personal experience that occurred in Chicago.

When I was a boy, I learned that one of the ways to have more fun rooting for my team was to have another team to hate with a passion. For me, that team was the Chicago Cubs. Everyone is familiar with the futility of the Cubs franchise; they have not won a World Series since 1908. Yet despite my disdain for the "Northsiders," my wife and I have always enjoyed going to Chicago to watch Cardinals/Cubs games, and the summer of 1987 was no exception.

Earlier that year I had gone to spring training and seen a young player by the name of Jim Lindeman rip

*Jim Grillo at Wrigley Field.* (Photograph courtesy of Jim Grillo)

the cover off the ball for a week. Even his outs seemed to be lined shots right at the defense, and it was obvious someone on the team would have to be traded to make room for him on the 25-man roster. That someone was Andy Van Slyke, who was sent to the Pirates as part of a deal for catcher Tony Peña.

So there I was in the "Friendly Confines" of Wrigley Field, and anyone who has been there knows that they have seats with an aisle right in front where fans wander by and sometimes obscure the view of action on the field. This particular afternoon was reminicent of a hot, muggy day in St. Louis, with temperatures in the 90s and very high humidity. As I settled into my seat with a cold beverage and a hot dog, bright red Cardinal cap perched on my head, I was startled by someone yelling "Hey!" right in front of me.

I looked up to see a large man, blocking the sun like the moon during a solar eclipse, with two bratwursts smothered in sauerkraut and dripping with mustard in one hand, and a large cup of beer in the other. His faded blue Cubs T-shirt had turned black from perspiration, and beads of moisture ran down his cheeks and off of his walrus-like mustache, dripping to the ground in front of me. His dirty Cubs hat rested precariously on a head that was as big as a basketball.

He looked down at me and in a thick Chicago accent made famous by George Wendt on "Saturday Night Live," said, *Andy Van Slyke for Tony Peña? What's the deal with that?"*

I swallowed the bite of hot dog I had been chewing, looked into his sweaty face, and answered calmly, "Lou Brock for Ernie Broglio."

The man's expression went blank as he fidgeted for something to say, and after what must have seemed to him like hours he blurted out, "Oh, yeah." He turned and waddled away, the memories of 80 years without a championship weighing heavily on his shoulders.

As I've grown older, I've learned that feeling hate

for the Cubs is a little much, but I will always root against them. In 1998 I followed the Cards with my son and daughter, and the three of us cheered for Mark McGwire as he established a new single-season home run record of 70. While we watched, I couldn't help but think how ironic it was that Mark's rival in the home run chase was the Cubs' Sammy Sosa. And in typical Northsider fashion, Sammy hit 66 homers that season with no record to show for it.

*John Mosher*  FLORISSANT, MISSOURI

## "One Fabulous Game"

The ecstasy and the agony of being a baseball fan is best illustrated by the games at the end of a season. You wait and hope from the early days of spring training that your team (in my case the Cardinals) will be in the pennant race at the end of September. When it finally happens, along with the joy you anticipated comes a feeling in the pit of your stomach as you realize your team might lose, and each game is so terribly important.

I want to tell you about one game in September 1974 that stands out to me as a great game; it's one that held all the feeling described above. The final score was 13-12, which tells you it was a game with much action.

The contest was played on September 25 as the season drew to a close. The Pirates led the Cardinals by one-half game, so the team that won would be in first place with six games remaining. Pittsburgh had taken the first two games of this series in St. Louis to come from one and a half games back to one-half game in front. The Bucs had a very good team and they had momentum.

The Pirates jumped on the Cardinals' young right-hander Bob Forsch for five runs in the first. Forsch was gone after only one-third of an inning and with him, it seemed, went our chances in this game and the pennant race. The gloom turned to great joy in the bottom of the third, however, when the Cardinals staged a six-run rally with some great names from the team's past contributing. Lou Brock started the rally, followed with hits by Ted Sizemore, Reggie Smith, Joe Torre and Ted Simmons. Two more hits, by Ken Reitz and Jose Cruz, completed the six-run inning.

To drive home the point of how vital this game was, when the Pirates scored in the fifth inning to tie the game at 6–6, the Cardinals brought in their left-handed relief ace, Al Hrabosky. The Cardinals put three runs on the board in the bottom of the fifth to go ahead 9–6, highlighted by a two-run homer by Reitz. The Pirates struck back with two in the sixth to close to 9–8. The Cardinals and Hrabosky held on tenaciously until the ninth inning, and one could almost taste the victory.

But a feeling of impending doom descended on me when the Pirates tied the game in the ninth on a throwing error by center fielder Bake McBride, the team's only error of the game. The gloom thickened when the Cardinals left two men stranded in the bottom of the ninth.

In the 11th inning Hrabosky, who pitched six and a third innings of relief and fanned nine, many at crucial times, weakened and was knocked out in a three-run Pirate rally. I continued to listen, in part because I didn't have the strength to turn off the game. A three-run rally didn't seem possible. Ted Sizemore singled to start the Cardinals' 11th. Reggie Smith walked, and

Ted Simmons drove Sizemore home with a single. Joe Torre then bounced to Rennie Sennett, the Pirates' second baseman, who had an easy play at first but threw wildly. The tying runs scored. The Cardinals then put in a speedy pinch runner for Torre, Larry Herndon, who scored the winning run on a sacrifice fly by Jim Dwyer, a good pinch hitter who could hit the ball when we needed it.

The joy and sense of relief was profound! The reason this game perhaps doesn't live in the memories of Cardinal fans as many others do is that the Pirates outplayed the Cardinals the final six games that season and won the pennant by one game. But this game reinforced to me not to give up on my team, for in the words of the great Cardinal pitcher and philosopher Joaquin Andujar, "You never know!"

## Rick Geissal ST. LOUIS

In 1946, my father—then 20 years old—had a ticket for the seventh game of the World Series. His uncle, John "Moon" Mullen—then only about 35 years old, but a much older man than my youthful father—begged my dad for the ticket. My dad did not want to part with it, but Moon insisted that, *since he was so old*, he might well die before the Cardinals were ever in another World Series. My dad relented, given this perspective, and gave him the ticket. That was the game when Enos Slaughter scored all the way from first base on a single to win the Series!

By the way, Uncle Moon lived many years, saw many other Cardinal pennant winners, and my dad never forgot!

# *Mark Rubin*   OLIVETTE, MISSOURI

I've been a Cardinal fan for all of my 31 years and then some, as I attended a game of the 1967 World Series when my mother was pregnant with me. Since then, the passion has continued, and I've experienced a lot of highs and lows. The pinnacle was Game Seven of the 1982 World Series. I was lucky enough to be sitting seven rows behind the Cardinals' dugout on that frigid night. Although my mother (the second-biggest baseball fan in the family) wouldn't let her 14-year-old son run onto the field after the victory (a parenting flaw of which I remind her frequently), the unbelievable drama of that ninth inning was unmatched.

Fans were dangling from the outfield walls, ready to swarm the turf, as Bruce Sutter battled Milwaukee's Gorman Thomas for the final out. Thomas fouled off one two-strike pitch after another, and I couldn't help but wonder what would happen if Gorman hit one off the wall or, more likely, some Cardinals fan's backside. I've never felt more jubilation than when strike three ended the Series and the season. The subsequent celebration and symphony of honking horns capped a magical evening.

A few negative memories are scattered among the good, most of these involving bad trades, bad seasons, or bad games. Perhaps the worst occurred in 1996. I happened to be traveling to Alabama the day the

*Mark Rubin, left, and his sister Laura with Cardinal pitcher Bob Sykes, in 1980. The following year, Sykes was traded to the New York Yankees for future MVP Willie McGee.* (Photograph courtesy of Mark Rubin)

Cards were facing the Braves in Game Seven of the NLCS, and my mother and I took the two-hour side trip to Atlanta and that forgettable contest.

We got to our upper-deck seats well before the first pitch and watched the pre-game preparations of that night's St. Louis starter, Donovan Osborne. He wasn't prepared. Soon after the game began, we were surrounded by 50,000 tomahawk-chopping Braves fans, watching a blowout. As disappointing as that game was, however, it capped a great inaugural season for Tony La Russa and wonderful farewell year for Ozzie Smith.

So many memories, win and lose, but my experiences during the 1987 season remain among my fondest recollections. That fall, I was a college student in Austin, Texas. I had several buddies at school who were also from the St. Louis area, with whom I followed the pennant race. We had a routine: Each night, we'd get into my car, tune the radio to KMOX, and drive until the reception became clear. One evening, when the Cards were facing the Mets, Terry Pendleton hit a timely home run to center field off of Roger McDowell. My friend Ted and I were in my car when that happened, and if it hadn't been a compact, we would have done back flips. Instead, we began a wild series of high fives, screams, and bounces off of the seats.

Most Cardinal fans remember that home run as a key to the season—it helped propel us past the "Pond Scum" New York club and the rest of our division. We won the NL pennant, and went on to face the Minnesota Twins in the World Series. On the night of Game Seven, my St. Louis contingent and I were prepared (and perhaps overconfident?). We'd purchased five bottles of champagne for a post-game celebration. Unfortunately, the Cardinals didn't cooperate, so we were unable to implement our initial plan of spraying one another while our victorious team did the same thing in the Metrodome clubhouse. Instead, we put the beverage to its intended use, and toasted the team and the season, commiserating as only college students can.

# *Tim Woodburn* LEXINGTON, KENTUCKY

## "My 60 Seconds with Jack Buck Re-Energized My Dream"

A s a child growing up in South St. Louis County, I sometimes had a bit of a behavior problem. And when it came time for my parents to dish out the punishment, they knew how to hit home. They would not ground me from going outside or playing with friends. Instead, I would first get grounded from the radio or television, preventing me from following my beloved baseball team. During those times, I would volunteer to go to bed early, around 7:30 P.M., in order to sneak my transistor radio under my pillow and listen to the man whom I considered my personal friend, though we had never met, Jack Buck. My parents couldn't understand why a kid who always wanted to stay up as late as possible would suddenly perform a 180. It took them a few years to figure it out.

My favorite toy as a child was my tape recorder, and I was constantly practicing calling baseball and hockey. When I graduated from high school, I enrolled in broadcast journalism school to chase a lifelong sports broadcasting dream. As I grew older, however, I began to recognize the intimidating path that lay ahead if I were to pursue this dream—huge competition, low wages at first, paying dues, making contacts.

My junior year at the University of Missouri–

Columbia was also my third consecutive summer of vending soda and beer at Busch Stadium during Cardinal games. I wore a ridiculous yellow, red and blue outfit, sweated my tail off running up and down steps, and traveled 120 miles each way every home baseball weekend just to have an association with the Cardinals. I worked with my best friend in life, the current Reverend William Kapp. We never vended after the seventh inning, instead settling in with nachos and soda in some obscure corner to watch the end of every game. Those were the lean years, '88, '89 and '90, when the Redbirds were very average. It didn't matter. It was the Cardinals and we felt a part of the whole experience.

As I matured and further realized the daunting path I had chosen, I began to second-guess my stubborn pursuit of a broadcasting career. One lazy, hot, humid Sunday in 1990 I was walking in my Sport-Service clown suit around Busch Stadium, en route to the vendors' den. Just the day before, I'd had a talk with my father about perhaps changing my major to pre-law. As I turned a corner, a man approached me and I nonchalantly stepped out of the way in passing. When I looked up, I immediately recognized the crooked smile and white mop of Jack Buck. At first I was stunned, and I think he saw that I was a bit off-guard as he said, "Hiya doin?" He didn't keep walking, but stopped. It was as if time stood still for a long 60 seconds as I complimented him on his on-air performance and, feeling somewhat embarrassed wearing the SportService uniform, indicated to him that I was pursuing a similar career.

Buck asked me what kinds of things I was doing to get my foot in the door, and recommended I volunteer and get something on my résumé besides my address: "Make it your top priority. The field's wide open. You'll never regret it if you do what's necessary to get that first job. Good luck, kid." He slapped me on the back and moved on. It is the only conversation I have ever had with the man.

Re-inspired, I returned to campus that weekend and immediately pursued a volunteer DJ shift at a campus station. Night hours. I got on. Within weeks, I co-hosted a weekly sports show. Then I DJed at a skating rink to smooth out my delivery in front of kids who'd never remember me. Next, the news job at a radio station. Then the news and eventually sports job at the TV station (all volunteer).

Finally, I made the difficult decision to move back with my parents so I could volunteer as an intern with the St. Louis Blues' PR department. I constructed a résumé play-by-play tape. I got my first play-by-play job in Birmingham, Alabama; I then moved to Virginia and now Kentucky, where I am in my eighth season of calling professional hockey play-by-play in the American Hockey League. I also co-anchor a weekly television show on a CBS affiliate and co-host a top-rated morning show and weekly call-in sports open line.

I was literally hours away from changing my major prior to a chance meeting. Today, I wake up every morning and love my career. Thanks, Jack. I'm sure he doesn't remember me, but that is what makes the gesture all the more Hall-of-Fame.

## *Mike Ray*   BRANSON, MISSOURI

I was seven years old when I saw my first Cardinals game in 1964. The Cards were something like 13 games out in August and beat the first-place Phillies the day we went. We lived several hours from St. Louis. After the game, I begged my dad to bring me to another game that year. As he told the story, he looked down at me and somehow just couldn't say no, although he really didn't want to do it. So, he had a bright idea. He told me he'd bring me to another game that year *if* the Cardinals got into first place (of course thinking he was totally safe since they were well out of it late in the season and were trailing several teams). Well, as fate had it, the Phillies collapsed and the Cardinals got hot and went into a tie for first with three or four games left. I woke him up at 4:30 A.M. the next morning and said, "Let's go." He tried to bribe me, but it was no use. He got up, we drove to St. Louis, and the Cards went on to win the World Series.

That was many years ago. I have a family of my own now, and I took them to the August 13, 1997, game at Busch Stadium. The Cards were playing the New York Mets, and when they stuck us with three runs in the first I found myself thinking, "Oh, no. Not one of *those* games." But then Mark McGwire came up to bat in the bottom of the inning with a man on base. My son Adam's eyes came alive. After Mac swung and missed, I told Adam to remember that no ballplayer gets a hit every time. He looked at me in disbelief and said, "Dad, he's gonna hit a homer. No doubt." I turned to watch another pitch and BOOM—upper deck! We went wild.

McGwire had another home run and a single that night. Unfortunately, he struck out in the 10th and the Mets won the game. Afterwards, we were waiting for my wife to return from the ladies' room. As the crowd streamed by, I looked down and noticed that Adam was crying, although he was trying to hide it. When I asked him what was wrong, he said, "I hate the Mets." I told him teams have players from everywhere, that the Mets even have a player from St. Louis, and all the teams are just trying to do their best. That's what makes baseball so much fun. He said he didn't care; they should have let McGwire hit another homer anyway. Looking down at him, the tears in his eyes under a shiny new red batting helmet, I found myself getting a little misty as well. I remember a few years ago another boy was at the ballpark with his dad, saying much the same thing. Now my dad is gone, but these bittersweet baseball memories will never leave me.

# Kim and Curt Turner

ST. PETERS, MISSOURI

Kim: On an unexpected evening off, my friend and co-worker Julie invited me to join her at a Cardinals' game. A group of five of us went, and upon arriving headed toward our customary spot in the right-field bleacher section. I decided to stop at the refreshment stand and meet up with everyone at our seats. Julie saw me searching and came over to get me. She happened to stop right in front of a handsome young man sitting alone in the first row of the upper section. I could not help but notice him as he fit my well-known description of the "ideal guy"—red hair, green eyes, and an athletic build. I glanced up at him and smiled, but walked away. Taking our seats behind right field, we could see my favorite player, Rex Hudler, directly in front of us. Seeing him made me think again of the man in the stands, a Rex look-alike.

Curt: I was living in Chicago at the time. While visiting my uncle in Springfield, Illinois, I realized I was only two hours away from Busch Stadium. I always sit in the left-field bleachers because of my childhood admiration for Lou Brock. That day, however, for some unknown reason, I wandered over to the right-field side. All I wanted to do was watch the game.

Kim: After some teasing from my friends, I decided to invite the man in the stands to join us. No luck. He simply smiled when I made the hasty invitation on my way to the concession stand. I returned to my seat, but we continued to exchange a few glances.

Curt: At that moment, then-Expos Delino De-Shields and Marquis Grissom were punishing the Cardinals. I was focused on the game.

Kim: Again I endured teasing and responded to the challenge. I walked over, stood right in front of his seat and introduced myself. We talked for about ten minutes, but it was clear that his interest was on the game. He told me his name, that he lived in Chicago and that in college he'd played ball with one of the Expos. All too soon my friends came over and said they were ready to leave. I hoped that Curt would ask for my phone number, but he did not.

Curt: The first time I actually looked into her eyes was when we said good-bye. I was stunned. Kim has the most beautiful cat-like green eyes I have ever seen. Her friends dragged her away and I did nothing.

Kim: As we drove home I had a sinking feeling in my stomach. I felt as if I had walked away from something very important and could not figure out how to fix it. Later that night I dreamed Curt had noticed that one of the ushers, Katie Fenton, knew us and would attempt to contact me through her. I told three people about this dream; they thought I was crazy.

Curt: After the game I started the drive back to Springfield. Heading north on I-55, I realized that the Cardinals were playing the following night. I turned around and checked into a motel in Collinsville. The

*Kim and Curt Turner celebrate at their rehearsal party with Katie Fenton and fellow usher.* (Photograph courtesy of the Turners)

next evening, sitting in the same spot in right field, I figured Kim might show up a gain. No luck. I also couldn't find the usher who appeared to know her the night before. I was trapped in the bleachers until the seventh inning when the gates opened to the rest of the ballpark. I was the first person to exit. I knew that my only chance was to find the missing usher and my search began with only two innings left. Soon it was the bottom of the ninth. I had circled Busch Stadium two and one-half times already. Where was she? Maybe she had the night off. I heard the crowd applauding something on the field, but I had work to do. Finally, I found her working the guest relations booth.

*Kim and Curt cut the groom's cake, a replica of Busch Memorial Stadium.* (Photograph courtesy of the Turners)

I explained the situation to her and she agreed to pass on my phone number. All of a sudden Bernard Gilkey cracked a homer and the Cards won.

Kim: Two days after the game, I was working my part-time job at Kennelwood when the phone rang. It was Katie with a message for me, Curt's phone number in Chicago! We could not believe that my dream had actually come true. I called him the next day, and we have been together ever since.

Curt: Ten days later I returned to St. Louis for our first date. This time I wasn't sitting alone in the bleachers. It was the first of many games we continue to attend together.

Kim: To celebrate our fateful meeting at the game, we held our rehearsal party in the right-field bleachers. Our families met for the first time there in the stands, just as Curt and I had nine months earlier. The next day, April 24, 1993, two wedding cakes were delivered at the reception—one a traditional white cake, the other a replica of Busch Stadium. We wrote to thank the Cardinals for playing such an important part in our lives, and received a letter of congratulations from Joe Torre that is now a permanent part of our wedding album.

# *Ann Edwards*  PADUCAH, KENTUCKY

My husband and I have been Cardinal fans all of our lives. I grew up in the bootheel of Missouri, and my parents listened to all of the Cardinals' games on the radio; it was an integral part of life. Our rare trip to St. Louis and a ball game was the highlight of each summer. In fact, one of my clearest memories from childhood is visiting my grandmother in Fayette one hot summer day, and hearing a Redbird game (with Dizzy Dean pitching) wafting through the air from both her house and my uncle's house across the street.

Gene, my husband, moved to St. Louis from Kentucky when he was 16. He'd already been a fan, but his love for Cardinal baseball was further solidified by finally being able to see many games. When we married, after a year in Guam, we moved to St. Louis and went to the ballpark as often as we could with four small boys. When that wasn't possible, we listened to KMOX. It was quite natural, then, that our boys would grow up loving Cardinal baseball. That didn't change when we moved to Paducah in 1963, as most people here are also ardent Cardinal fans. Certainly we continued to be and have shared season tickets for a number of years now.

In 1968 I was expecting our sixth child. I had told my children that if the baby was a boy, they could name him. I knew they were sure to select the name of a favorite athlete, more than likely a Cardinal. I had one concern about this, however. The Cards' first baseman that year was Orlando Cepeda. He was an outstanding player and the idol of my children. However, I wasn't sure that the name "Orlando" was my first choice. But, a promise is a promise. Fortunately, the kids had another player they also admired, and the name they chose was Timothy, after catcher Tim McCarver. I was extremely pleased, for he was also one of our favorites.

My son Tim has always been very proud of his name and how he got it. When he was in elementary school, we went to St. Louis to see the Cards play the Phillies. By this time, McCarver had been traded to Philadelphia. We took a baseball with us, hoping we might somehow get it signed for Tim by his namesake. We struck up a conversation with an attendant, who happened to have a son in Paducah. We told him the story of our Tim's name, and how we hoped to get an autograph from McCarver. The usher told us he would relay our tale to the catcher, and get him to sign the ball. McCarver did sign it, with a wonderful personal message. It is a kindness that our Tim will never forget.

# *Keith Carver*  ST. LOUIS

My defining moment as a Cardinal fan came the day after the Redbirds won the '82 Series. I'd had a single ticket to Game Seven but was instructed—make that threatened—by my boss that I had better be out of town seeing customers or my carcass was toast. Thus, I watched that final game in a sports bar in Macomb, Illinois, with a clubful of misguided Cub fans. The next morning I had to drive from Macomb to Peoria for a meeting and while in the car I was listening to the morning show on KMOX. Lucky for me, the show's host replayed the final inning or so of Jack Buck's radio broadcast of the game. Even though I knew the outcome, each pitch tugged on my nerves like I was there live. My palms were sweaty. My heart was racing frantically. Finally, when Bruce Sutter struck out Gorman Thomas and Mr. Buck yelled, "That's a winner, a World Series winner for the Cardinals!" I began to bawl like a baby. There I was, in my car, alone with the corn fields, crying my eyes out. I wanted to jump up and hug someone, slap a high five, anything to share my excitement with others who felt as I did. No one was there so I pulled over, finished my cry, wiped the tears of joy from my cheeks and grinned ear to ear for the next hour, so happy and proud to be a Cardinal fan.

# Brian Gilmore   ST. LOUIS

To me, Cardinal baseball is much more than a spring-to-fall hobby. It is the source of my joy, my sadness, and my frustrations. If I had the choice to do anything in the world, attending a Cardinal baseball game would be high up on my list.

My all-time favorite game, which I was lucky enough to attend, was Game Four of the 1996 NLCS against the Atlanta Braves, Cards leading the best-of-seven series two games to one. Behind Denny Neagle, Atlanta was dominating. Going into the bottom of the seventh, Neagle had allowed only a harmless single, and the Braves were up 3–0. Neagle got Brian Jordan and Gary Gaetti right away. Two outs, no one on. Then the most exciting sequence of my young Cardinal life happened. John Mabry hit a single. Tom Pagnozzi followed that up with a walk. Bobby Cox then decided to take out Neagle and go to Greg McMichael. With almost everyone in the stadium expecting Ozzie Smith to pinch-hit for the pitcher, Tony La Russa gambled and sent in rookie Dmitri Young, who had just 30 big-league at-bats. After laying off three straight change-ups, "Big D" hit a fastball off the center-field fence for a triple, doing a belly flop as he rumbled into third. Busch was rockin'. Then Royce Clayton drove in Dmitri with an infield single, tying the game. Little did we know, there would be more fireworks to come. With one out in the eighth, BJ hit the "shot heard 'round St. Louis," a go-ahead home run. Joe Buck later said that the booth was actually shaking. The Cards won 4–3. What a game—makes me proud to be a Cardinal fan.

## *Terry Chambers*   CRESTWOOD, MISSOURI

I saw Lou Brock, the "Base Burglar," play many times over the years and had the opportunity to meet him, on the field, on one occasion. The Schnucks grocery store chain sponsored a "Batboy/girl of the Day" contest and my then-eight-year-old daughter, Allyson, entered. She said on the form she wanted to win "so my daddy will be proud of me," and her entry was selected.

On the day of the game, Allyson, our sons Joe and Andy, my wife, Virginia, and Granny and I were met at the stadium by Joe Cunningham, who gave Allyson a team-autographed ball and escorted us on a tour of the clubhouse. The tour ended suddenly in the dugout. Joe disappeared and there we stood alone, practically on the field, wondering what to do next. The game was just minutes away and the players were warming up in front of the dugout, playing catch (if big leaguers play catch). They all had on their game faces (Boy, did Ted Simmons *ever* have his on!) and were unaware of this family standing there.

Somehow, through that sea of players and flying balls, Lou and I made eye contact. In an instant Lou stopped and made his way to where we standing. He introduced himself, grabbed Bake McBride and several other players, brought them over and introduced them. He talked with us until he had to take the field.

Lou didn't ask who the Chambers family was or even why we were there. I think he just saw us looking lost and came over to offer comfort. When he left the dugout, those smiling eyes were burned forever in my memory and he left me grateful for the impression he'd made on Allyson. Joe returned and escorted us to our seats.

How do you measure a man? By the home runs he hits, the bases he steals, or by his impact and influence on people who could not possibly help him? Records are soon broken but impressions last a lifetime. Thanks to a truly Big Guy.

*The Chambers kids—Andy, Allyson and Joe—in the dugout with Lou Brock.* (Photograph courtesy of Terry Chambers)

# Hortense Zingsheim

UNIVERSAL CITY, TEXAS

I am 82 years old. On September 29, 1934, I started my first job as secretary to the manager of the Fairgrounds Hotel in North St. Louis. A few weeks later, the St. Louis Cardinals played the Detroit Tigers in the World Series. The Fairgrounds Hotel was located just three blocks from Sportsman's Park and was the scene of many fans from Oklahoma and Texas, where there was no Major League Baseball in those days. I recall arriving at work one morning and finding a hungover male fan sleeping on my desk— quite unrattling for a girl of 18.

During the next seven years, I knew many of the St. Louis Cardinals and Browns who lived at the hotel, among them Johnny Mize, Enos Slaughter and Don Padgett. I met many more through the manager of the concessions at Sportsman's Park, Blake Harper. He also lived at the Fairgrounds Hotel and had approached me about doing some clerical work for him. Gladly! I then had two jobs, one for him and one for the hotel. Through Mr. Harper, I was able to see many Cardinal games by mentioning his name at the press gate. Dizzy and Paul Dean were big attractions in those days and could fill the stands. If Dizzy was pitch-

*Hortense Simon and Cardinal Don Padgett take turns posing in front of his new Buick, circa 1938.* (Photographs courtesy of Hortense Zingsheim)

ing, I would leave the hotel early on weekdays in order to catch the last few innings.

Those were also the baseball years in which the three "M's"—Martin, Medwick and Mize—were a significant part. My favorite was Johnny Mize, but he married "the other girl." Don Padgett, Cardinal catcher and left fielder, was another favorite. He loved watermelon, and we often ate said delicacy together at Sam the Watermelon Man's place on Natural Bridge Avenue. When Don purchased his new Buick, he took me for a drive to Chain of Rocks Park before he had to report for that day's game. I introduced Don to my family in the course of our acquaintance, but he, too, married "the other girl." I was a two-time loser!

On Sunday mornings, some of the Cardinals and other locals would occasionally gather at Fairgrounds Park (across the street from the Fairgrounds Hotel) to play "stick ball." They batted with a broomstick and used a small cork ball to hit; I don't know how they hit it but they did!

Then there was Pepper Martin's makeshift band. They were a popular attraction for the team and very colorful. There was some doubt as to the quality of their music. As compared to that of today, however, they were a symphony, particularly on "The Wabash Cannonball," which I recall as Pepper Martin's favorite. I heard him singing it as he walked through the lobby of the hotel.

With a few misgivings, I departed the Fairgrounds Hotel to work at the DeSoto Hotel in downtown St. Louis. It was the summer of 1941—a foreshadowing of changing times, and our entrance into World War II. Of my seven-year association with Cardinal ballplayers, fans, hotel guests and my co-workers, I have the fondest of memories, and I am grateful for them. They were some of the best of my life.

## *Ryan May*    ORLANDO, FLORIDA

Last year, my mom, my sister and I went to Wal-Mart to see Ozzie Smith when he made a personal appearance there. When we got to the front of the line, Ozzie signed a picture for me and I said, "Thanks, man," and shook his hand. My mom took a picture of me with him and then said to Ozzie, "My son has been a fan of yours since he was two." Ozzie looked over at me and noticed I was dressed head to toe in Cardinal gear. He smiled and said, "Oh yeah? Alright!" My sister got her autograph and picture, and then Ozzie asked if I wanted to take *another* picture with him. I walked over, *he stood up, leaned across the table* and shook my hand for the photo. Then, I told him I had his special retirement ball (the red one) with me, and he asked, "Do you want me to sign that for you?" I said, "Sure!" He signed it, handed the ball back to me, and shook my hand again. My mom walked away with tears in her eyes, and I was shaking with excitement. He actually stopped and spent time with us. He is the nicest guy ever, and it was one of the greatest experiences of my life so far. By the way, the picture turned out *great*, too.

*Cardinal legend Ozzie Smith shakes hands with Ryan May.* (Photograph courtesy of Ryan May)

*Dan Ganey*   CARBONDALE, ILLINOIS

Having been born on the east side of the river from St. Louis, I have been a Cardinal fan for as long as I can remember, but my two most cherished "Cardinal moments" occurred in the '90s. The first was when I, along with my two older brothers, attended a Randy Hundley Fantasy Camp at Busch Stadium in July 1994. I chose 14, Ken Boyer's uniform number. (My favorite player as a kid was Ken Boyer because he played third base and so did I. In my Ken Boyer batting stance I hit many home runs in our driveway Whiffle ball games.) The camp was three days of sore muscles and pure joy, culminating in a Sunday morning game between the campers and the Old Timers. And who should arrive to pitch for the Old Timers? Why, none other than Hall of Fame hurler Bob Gibson. When it was my turn to bat, I dug in, looked to the mound, and quietly said to myself, "My God! That's Bob Gibson!" I watched him paint the outside corner at my knees with the first pitch. He and Randy Hundley, who was catching, both chided me for taking the pitch and told me to "take a hack." So I hit the next pitch to the wall in right field for a triple and two RBIs. Unfortunately for my brother Mike, who was up to bat next, Gibby is still a competitor. He struck out my brother and showed our family who was boss.

My second most-cherished moment happened when Mark McGwire hit his 62nd home run of the 1998 season. The memory isn't solely related to the breaking of Roger Maris' record, but also to the pure, child-like joy he showed rounding the bases and hoisting his son into the air. As a baseball fan in general, a Cardinal fan in particular, and a father of my own two boys, that scene will be etched into my memory forever. It doesn't get any better than that!

# Charles R. Wooderson ST. LOUIS

## "My Two-Day Journey to Cardinal Fandom"

I
t all began on a Monday, the day before the seventh game of the 1946 World Series between the Cardinals and the mighty Boston Red Sox. I and three of my senior high school classmates, along with two parents, left Spickard, Missouri, by car for St. Louis to attend that deciding game. It was a spur-of-the moment decision. Prior to this, I was only casually interested in Cardinal baseball (high school basketball was my sports passion), and I'm not even sure I was aware of the Red Sox prior to the Series.

We arrived in St. Louis late Monday evening, checked into a motel, got up at 4 A.M. and had breakfast, then headed for Sportsman's Park. There we found the ticket line, several blocks long and five or six abreast. Being a naive country boy who had never attended a big-league sports event, it didn't enter my mind until hours later that there were a finite number of tickets available, and the last one might sell before we could buy ours. I remember the nervous concern, even a tinge of fear, as we crept closer and closer to the booth. Would the tickets hold out? Would the 300-mile trip be for nothing? I caught myself crowding closer to the person ahead of me as if that might, somehow, get us to that booth before the last tickets sold. Then, finally, with profound relief, I slipped my money under the bars of the window. I had a ticket! We all had tickets! But I will never forget: As I was making my purchase, the small door at the back of the booth opened, and someone asked the clerk how many tickets he had left. He replied, "Seven." Had we arrived in line 30 seconds later than we did, early that morning, we would surely have been too late.

That Tuesday afternoon, we saw the Cardinals pull off one of the great upsets in World Series history. Watching Harry Brecheen become the first left-handed pitcher ever to win three games in one World Series, and Enos Slaughter make his famous eighth-inning run from first to home on a short double by Harry Walker, engraved the Cardinals forever into my sports psyche.

# *Bill Stunkel* ST. PETERS, MISSOURI

While working as a PBX installer for Southwestern Bell Telephone, I worked at Busch Stadium for 17 years, in the offices of the baseball and football Cardinals. When Mr. Bob Howsam was general manager of the baseball Cardinals, he requested a special assembly phone installed in his L-shaped desk. This had to be made at the Western Electric plant in Chicago, and took some length of time.

When the equipment was received, I talked to Mr. Joe McShane, business manager for the team, about installing the phone and making sure it would fit the space provided. This took place on a Friday. He suggested we wait until the following Monday.

Over the weekend Mr. Howsam was made general manager of the Cincinnati Reds, and Stan Musial was named general manager of the Cardinals.

On Monday I talked again with Mr. McShane about installing the equipment, and asked if he thought Mr. Musial would want it. He said, "Let's go in and see Mr. Musial and explain it to him," so we did. After I went through the details of the special assembly with Mr. Musial, he replied, "You mean I get a phone with this job?"

## Erin Seals ST. LOUIS

My favorite memory of going to a Cardinals game is from a few Augusts ago, when I won tickets from a local library reading program. My family went on my mom's birthday, August 21. We had nosebleed seats, but that didn't matter. We were enjoying the game, but the Cardinals were losing. We were patient until the bottom of the ninth. Then my dad sighed and opted for us to leave. My sister and I insisted that we stay; something exciting could happen. During the bottom of the ninth, with two outs and the bases loaded, my favorite player, Brian Jordan, came up to bat. The count went to three balls and two strikes. Then, the pitcher threw, and Brian Jordan's bat connected with the ball. We all stood up. Was it? Yes! It was! Brian Jordan hit a grand slam to win the game! I turned to my mom and said, "That was for you."

*David E. Altom*  FERGUSON, MISSOURI

I t was 1964. Late in the season. The Phillies were fading. The Cards were surging. Philadelphia came to St. Louis for a series and my mom and dad took me to one of the games. We sat in the screened-in area behind right field. During the game, a man a few seats over from us began to heckle the Phillies' right fielder, number six. "Hey, Number Six, move over a little to your left! Hey, Number Six! Move over!"

This continued throughout the game. In a later inning, the Cardinals rallied. Men on first and third. The batter hit a screamer to the left of the right fielder. He took two steps to his left and dove for the ball, just missing. The ball went all the way to the wall. Both runners scored. The Cards took the lead.

After the crowd noise subsided, the heckler called out, "Hey, Number Six! I told you to move over to your left!"

We all broke up. To this day I wonder, who was that guy? And who was Number Six?

[Editor's note: Right fielder Johnny Callison wore number six for the Phillies in 1964.]

## Beverly Jaegers

### "The Red-Headed League"

Sportsman's Park was a mecca for St. Louisans in those long-ago summer days during World War II. Its looming grandstands held many memories for those of us who grew up in St. Louis in the days when the ballpark crowned Grand Avenue. My dad, Jerome Weingart, was a St. Louis policeman, as his father had been, and a longtime baseball fan. We had lived for years just up the street from Stan Musial, but none of us had ever met any other ballplayer.

When I was almost nine, we managed to get a car, and after that would go down to the ballpark on summer days, and when we could, some evenings as well. I can still remember the taste of those hot dogs and mugs of root beer, a taste that has never been matched by anything else I could eat. One night my mother, Garnet Weingart, was watching one of the ballplayers practice on the field. Picking up my small brother, she went down the aisle to the grandstand rail next to the dugout on the third-base side. Mother had lovely dark auburn hair just like movie star Maureen O'Hara's, and my brother, Jerry, had what you might politely refer to as fiery orange hair. She held Jerry, Jr., up in the grandstand lights, and waited a few minutes until the ballplayer looked over at her.

*Beverly with little brother (and Red Schoendienst look-alike) Jerry, in 1942.* (Photograph courtesy of Beverly Jaegers)

She smiled and waved at him, and he came over to the grandstand and grinned at my brother. He shook Jerry's hand, as well as my mother's, patted the boy's head, and they talked for a few minutes. I was mystified, as I knew she didn't know any ballplayer other than Stan Musial, who was out on the field.

Soon the game was ready to begin, and the ballplayer stepped away from the fence, smiled and took off his cap. As he did so, I saw that his own hair was as red as my brother's. What a big surprise that was!

My mom took little Jerry down to the third-base rail many times when we attended games in that old park and Red Schoendienst was as friendly and as gracious as his teammate Stan Musial. Schoendienst always came to the fence and talked to my brother and my mom. Redheads do seem to belong to a league of their own.

I now have two redheaded granddaughters of *my* own, and maybe, someday, we will be at Busch Stadium, and Red Schoendienst will come walking out on the field and . . . Or maybe, just maybe, it might be Mark McGwire.

# *Aaron Greenberg*  ST. LOUIS

My father took me to my first game in 1937, a Cardinals-Cubs doubleheader, and I've been a rabid fan since my days as a member of the Knot Hole Gang. In fact, I still have my Knot Hole Card, issued in 1942. The Gang was invented by the new Cardinal owners in 1917. It was originally started to reduce juvenile delinquency, but was later enlarged to include many school-age children through the YMCA. Spaces in the left-field stands were reserved for us Knotholers. These were a couple of the Knot Hole Gang rules: "1) I will not at any time miss school to attend a game; 2) I will uphold the principles of clean speech, clean sports, and clean habits, and will stand with the rest of the Gang against cigarettes and profane language in the stands and off the field."

Much in baseball has changed since the 1930s and '40s. Back then, players could not be free agents and therefore were not paid enormous salaries. More players played "for the love of the game." Players used to leave their gloves on the field, and the bats were on the ground in front of the dugouts. The outfield fences were not as flexible as they are today; poor Pete Reiser had a short career because he kept running into the fences. Baseball games were not broadcast on Sundays.

One of the great consistencies in Cardinal baseball

throughout the years has been the game announcers. France Laux, Harry Caray, Gabby Street, Joe Garagiola, Mike Shannon and, of course, Jack Buck— we have had many wonderful broadcasters over the years. It's much easier for me to follow the Cardinals these days, with *all* games being broadcast on the radio, and most of them televised. During the Great Depression and World War II, baseball was a great diversion for fans. And it still is. I've enjoyed a near lifetime of Cardinal baseball.

*Rick Geissal*   ST. LOUIS

In 1964, my cousin Jack McCarthy was the weather guy on a TV station in Peoria, Illinois, where my parents and I lived. Like me, Jack was a big Cardinal fan. The sports guy on that channel was Bob Starr— later a Cardinals' announcer, and then the California Angels' announcer for many years. Bob was a huge Yankees' fan, which came into play when the two teams met in the World Series that year.

In those days, the TV station had a transparent weather map out on the sidewalk in front of the station. When Jack did the weather report, one could see the people walking past. It was neat. It added something to the forecast, and probably the ratings, as well.

During that World Series, Jack and Bob teased one another unmercifully, depending on whose team won that day. Jack had quite a time with Bob the day Ken Boyer hit a grand slam to beat the Yanks 4–3 and tie up the Series 2–2.

On the day the Cardinals won, Jack was doing his weather report—out on the sidewalk—when a hearse pulled up and stopped directly behind the weather map. The window shades were drawn, and draped across a casket, for all to see, was a banner that read, "Yankees." It capped it all off for me!

## *Derek Adams* ST. ANN, MISSOURI

My first contact with Cardinal players came when I was about 10. We had great seats on the first-base side of Busch Stadium, where the Cardinal bullpen was at the time. Greg Mathews had just finished playing catch with Tommy Herr and started signing autographs. I'd brought an old rubber baseball that had a large "X" marked on it. It was all that I had for players to sign. When I handed it to Greg, he took a long look at it, handed it back to me, reached into his glove and pulled out the ball with which he and Tommy had been playing catch. He signed it, "To Derek—Best wishes, Greg Mathews" and gave it to me. Wow! That made my day. I was also able to get Vince Coleman's and Ray Soff's autographs on that ball the same afternoon.

I cherished the ball so much that when we went out of town, I would take it with me, and I'm glad I did. One weekend we went camping and before we left I forgot to turn off my electric blanket. It malfunctioned, caught on fire, and burned my entire room to the ground. Thank God I had the ball with me. It is one of a few things from my childhood that did not burn. Now I keep it in a fireproof safe. I don't ever want to lose that ball.

## *Tom Heidger*  ARNOLD, MISSOURI

In August of 1971, this 14-year-old was bedridden with an ailment I cannot recall, possibly strep throat, but at any rate, I had a high fever and slept virtually around the clock for a couple of days. On one of those days, late on a Saturday afternoon, my dad gently woke me with the words, "Tommy, Gibson has a no-hitter going into the ninth. I thought you might want to listen to it." Whoa! Nothing short of death would have kept me down. For some reason, this weekend road game was not televised. I staggered into the kitchen, where the voice of Jack Buck emitted from the black radio atop the refrigerator. Bottom of the ninth. Two out. Willie Stargell at the plate. Strike three called!

# Jeff S. Pawlow   BELLEVILLE, ILLINOIS

## "It's in the Genes!"

While it's easy to assume that most baseball fans in St. Louis have Cardinal red blood pumping through their veins, I wonder if many have experienced four generations of Cardinal history like I have. This is the story of the Pawlow family, and how the love of our hometown team has intertwined itself with the love we have for each other.

As a third-generation Cardinal fan, I can vividly remember my Dad and "Pawp" telling me about "the good old days." "You mean Harry Caray wasn't always the announcer for the Cubs?" I asked after Dad and Pawp played some old record albums that featured the radio highlights from the 1964 and 1968 Cardinal seasons. I was also surprised to hear about Mike Shannon on the field instead of in the broadcast booth, and that Jack Buck was the color commentator as opposed to the play-by-play announcer. Holy Cow!

I was an eighth grader at the time, and we'd traveled to St. Louis from Pusan, South Korea, where my Dad was then stationed in the Air Force. We were staying with my grandparents in St. Louis, and had tickets to all of the home games for the '82 Series. We had traveled halfway around the world just to take in the Series and I was rarin' to go! While I was familiar with "Whiteyball," the Gashouse Gang, "Stan the Man" and "El Birdos" were foreign to me. This was about to change.

I recall Pawp and Dad telling me about how they used to listen to all of the Cardinals' games on a little orange radio that sat on the refrigerator in their house on Floy Avenue in the City of St. Louis. Pawp would help explain the play-by-play to my dad, and Dad would imagine that he was sitting in the stands at Sportsman's Park. After the game, Pawp would take Dad and his friends outside and divide everyone up into two teams for a pickup stickball game. Dad was always "Stan the Man" as he was the only lefty in the bunch.

Dad's most exciting experience was when Pawp took him to his first St. Louis Cardinals baseball game. Dad saw Stan Musial hit a home run and remembers that the game was rained out after four innings and had to be replayed. Dad's baseball stories went on and on (with Pawp keeping him honest) and it was obvious that the Cardinal genes had been successfully passed down from one generation to the next. Unfortunately, during those years, the Redbirds weren't winning.

According to Dad, 1964 was looking like more of the same. With about 10 games to play in the season, the Cardinals were seven or eight games behind the Phillies. Dad can remember sitting with Pawp like two little kids in front of their new hi-fi set as the Cardinals started to charge while the Phillies couldn't win. "I remember Harry Caray would stay at Sportsman's Park after the game was over and con-

*Three generations of Cardinal fans: Tom, Stan and Jeff Pawlow.* (Photograph courtesy of Jeff Pawlow)

tinue to broadcast the Phillies' game in the dark if it was not yet completed," said Dad. "We were all wondering if the miracle would continue, especially since we had tickets to the final game of the season."

The miracle did continue, and the Cardinals went on to capture their first NL pennant in 18 years with my grandparents, Dad and Mom (Dad's fiancée at the time) in the stands. Dad said, "It was my biggest thrill after waiting so long. I still remember all the cars honking and everyone celebrating as we left the park that Sunday afternoon."

After listening to Dad and Pawp recall their Cardinal memories, I was more excited than ever to get to the ballpark and Game One of the World Series.

*Jeff and Tom Pawlow pose with St. Louis General Manager Walt Jocketty (center) at the Cardinals' Roger Dean Stadium in Jupiter, Florida, during spring training 1999.* (Photograph courtesy of Jeff Pawlow)

Eight days later, we were at Busch Stadium and witnessed Bruce Sutter pitch the final strike of our World Series winner! I was hooked. The genes had been passed down again.

Attending high school in Cincinnati can be difficult for a Cardinal fan, especially when you're in the same class as Ken Griffey, Jr! It didn't matter to me, though, because the Cards were winning and slugging it out with the Mets for the NL East championship. I specifically remember Dad and I watching a Cards/Mets series late in the season during the height of our '80s rivalry with New York. Dad would go outside and pace on the driveway every time the Mets were up because, in his words, "nothing good can happen when the other team is at bat." I'd have to go out and collect him after the Cardinals recorded the third out each inning and then we'd watch the Cards bat in their half of the inning. Terry Pendleton's grand slam extinguished the Mets' fire and we were on our way to the playoffs again.

Perhaps the greatest Cardinal memory I have is the night I recorded an out for the Redbirds while attending a game at Riverfront Stadium. At the time, Dad was the Air Force commander at the General Electric plant in Cincinnati, and had developed a casual relationship with Reds' owner Marge Schott and player/manager Pete Rose, as they would visit the GE plant every year as part of their PR program. Mr. Rose would always give Dad a great deal of grief over the life-sized picture of him and Whitey Herzog hanging in his office, and always tried to convert us into Reds fans. Upon learning that we were being transferred back to the St. Louis area, Mrs. Schott invited all of us down to the game the next time the Cardinals were in town.

In the sixth inning of that game, with two outs and Barry Larkin on third, Eric Davis hit a towering foul ball that started drifting my way. The next thing I knew, I had leaned over the railing and caught the ball. The bad news was that Tony Peña was standing right below me and would have caught the ball if I hadn't interfered! Plate umpire John McSherry ruled fan interference and called Davis out. Score one for the Redbirds! Unfortunately, the whole event turned into a bit of a mini-controversy, as technically I should have been ejected from the game. Mrs. Schott wouldn't allow that and it stirred up a bit of a ruckus in Cincinnati. The video clip of the catch ended up being the "Play of the Day" and then made a second appearance during the pre-game show for NBC's "Game of the Week" the following Saturday. Needless to say, I still have the ball!

Today, I'm happily married to my wife, Cindy, who hails from the Kansas City area (which causes a bit of friction any time the 1985 Series is mentioned) and we have a two-and-a-half-year-old son named Stan (after "The Man"). Cindy has been reconditioned and is now a huge Cardinal fan who actually likes listening to Sports Open Line on KMOX. Maybe it has something to do with the Cardinal baseball cap she received at our rehearsal dinner, officially welcoming her to our family.

My biggest worry as a dad was that Stan wouldn't share my interest in the Cardinals. Luckily, this has not been the case. Stan loves crawling up on my lap to check the latest Cardinals score on the Internet, and already knows all of the words to "Take Me Out to the Ball Game." He's a huge Mark McGwire fan and jumps up and down anytime he witnesses a home run from Big Mac.

Which brings me to the conclusion of our story. While vacationing at Disney World with my extended family, we were wrapping up our first day at the Magic Kingdom when fireworks began going off overhead. Stan, who is a veteran of many Cardinal games, McGwire home runs, and the ensuing pyrotechnics, started jumping up and down and finally said, "Daddy, Daddy—Mark McGwire just hit a home run!" My dad looked at me and smiled. The genes had successfully been passed to a fourth generation. It doesn't get any better than that!

## *Sandy Duerr* VALLEY PARK, MISSOURI

My first real exposure to Cardinal baseball was in 1982, when I was almost 12 years old. The World Series was on at my house every night, and my parents and older brothers were glued to the TV. I didn't quite understand the game, though I had listened to a few games at my grandma's house. (She's the biggest Cards fan one could ever meet.) One evening, I decided to sit down and watch. I asked many questions as I followed along. I found myself very intrigued with this game, as intrigued as an 11-year-old could be, anyway.

Days later, I found myself searching for another game while playing Barbie dolls with a friend. Odd combination, Cardinal baseball and Barbies. My friend couldn't understand why I was watching this game; she had never been exposed to it, either. But from there on out, I watched every game of the '82 Series, getting hooked fast and understanding the game quickly. Will anyone who watched that Series ever forget the ending of Game Seven? Bruce Sutter seemed to me at the time to be a miracle worker of some sort. Once he came in, I knew the game was over. And I was quite fascinated with his split-fingered fastball. It looked so neat to me when they would show the close-up of his fingers. I'll never forget Darrell Porter charging the mound and wrapping his legs around Sutter—quite a sight! I remember being very jealous of one of my older brothers that night, because as soon as the game was over he went downtown to party on the streets. Granted, I didn't even know what partying was at the time, but I knew downtown had to be exciting with the Cards just winning the World Series.

Fifteen years later, I find myself just as much thrilled by the game. I feel like a kid all over again when the season really gets hot, as it did in '96, when we were only one game away from the World Series. Now, winters seem long, and fans like me count the days until spring training and opening day. There's just something about being in Busch Stadium. The craziness of the fans in the bleachers—that's what baseball is all about, to me. If the team doesn't go all the way, the games are still fun. The ballpark just has excitement in the air. And I do believe it even has a *smell* of excitement. I can only imagine how a ballplayer feels when he outdoes himself in a game— when a singles hitter knocks one out of the park, or when a home run hitter comes close to breaking a record. As a fan, every aspect of the game is exciting to me. What a sport, and what a city in which to enjoy it: St. Louis.

*Tom Thompson*   BALLWIN, MISSOURI

The year was 1971. I was 13 years old. My family took my best friend with us to the ball game. It was "Bat Night." During the national anthem, when the words ". . . and the home of the brave" were sung, my friend and I looked at each other and said, "No, home of the Cardinals!" In the bottom of the ninth inning, the Cardinals were rallying. They had the bases loaded, and Joe Torre was up to bat. The crowd was going crazy. All the kids were banging their new bats on the stadium floor, creating quite a racket. Torre hit a gapper, clearing the bases with a triple and winning the game.

Tuesday, September 8, 1998. We were watching the game on TV. I was holding my 12-day-old baby girl, Rachel, when Mark McGwire came up to bat. I turned Rachel so she could see the TV and said to her, "Look Rachel. McGwire is up to bat. Say 'Hit one for me, Mark. Hit one for Rachel.'" And, of course, he did.

# Jeff S. Kee  NASHVILLE, TENNESSEE

My grandfather was a Cardinal fan dating back to the days of the Gashouse Gang. He listened to every game on the radio—even after the advent of television—and as I was growing up, he regaled me with stories. He talked about the all-time greats he'd seen firsthand—Dizzy Dean on the mound, Medwick playing the field, and Stan Musial hitting like no one has since. He is the reason I am a Redbird fan. One of my favorite stories my grandfather told me involved the Cardinals' appearance in the 1934 World Series. Where my grandfather lived, it was very difficult to pick up the Cards' games on the radio. Grandpa found a station that was carrying the game, but reception was poor and he could barely make out the words. He had to place the radio near a window, and then keep his ear pressed against the speaker to decipher the play-by-play. He followed the entire World Series that way. Now that is a true fan. I can sympathize, because when I moved to east Tennessee, I could only get KMOX on my car radio. How many nights I have spent sitting in my car to follow the games.

I'm glad my grandfather got to see one last championship (1982) before he died in 1988. When he passed away, I buried my Cardinal hat in the casket with him. I went almost 10 years without owning another Redbird hat, but I finally broke down and bought one. I wore it recently when I watched the Birds play Atlanta, and I can never think of the team without thinking of him.

# *Fern Claas*   BEAUFORT, MISSOURI

My name is Fern Claas, and I am a quilter. What does being a quilter have to do with baseball? you might ask. Only the greatest experience of my life. The day after the Cardinals won the 1982 World Series, I started a quilt, at the suggestion of my daughter. The quilt commemorates the Series. Each player is depicted as a redbird seated on a bat, with a ball. Each player's name is on the bat, and his number is on the baseball. There is a bird for each player, coach, Whitey, and even Mr. Busch, whose bird is wearing a red cowboy hat. Darrell Porter's "bird" is roosting on a globe. I portrayed him as sitting on top of the world, literally, which I'm sure he was, having been named the Series' MVP. Also included in the quilt are Fredbird, a dugout, and the Clydesdales' hutch in harness. Atop the quilt are baseballs with the score of each game.

When the quilt was finished, a friend and I took it to the stadium. However, the team was still in spring training in Florida. We were asked to take it over to the newspaper office, where it was photographed, and the next day it was on the cover of the *St. Louis Globe-Democrat*. We were then invited to bring it to a baseball game, and there it was signed by every player. We met the team, and several players recalled seeing their grandmas quilting when they were little boys.

As a result of making this quilt, my family got to

*Fern Claas' 1982 World Series quilt.* (Photograph courtesy of Fern Claas)

see our very first baseball game in person. We live in a very small town, and this was the most exciting thing to ever happen to us. Now, I have 25 Redbirds to keep me warm when I get cold at night.

## Brian Hauck   MIAMI, OKLAHOMA

Since Brian Jordan signed a lucrative contract with the Atlanta Braves, I've heard some of my fellow fans criticize him. I would ask them:

Perhaps you've forgotten the way his hat would fly off as he rounded the bases on a triple?

Maybe you can't remember how aggressively he'd slide into second base on a stolen base attempt, and alertly bounce up, ready to continue to third?

Don't you remember the way he would literally fly around third base as he scored all the way from first?

How could you forget the way he'd crash into the outfield wall, risking life and limb to grab a fly ball, and refusing to allow an opponent that extra base hit?

Do you remember the shots of him standing on the dugout steps applauding a teammate's base hit . . . while the rest of the bench just sat there spitting seeds?

Or the way he'd run a hundred-yard dash to grab a foul ball?

Or the way he'd often come through for us with men on base?

Or the way he'd charge in toward the infield and dive for a ball, catch it, and slide across the grass?

Or dive for a ball and roll up to his feet ready to fire the ball to third base or home plate if a runner dared to challenge him?

Or his big smile?

Or his huge heart?

Or his always-dirty uniform?

There's a reason why a team like Atlanta coveted Brian Jordan. It may be a long time before the Cardinals organization produces another athlete of his caliber. Good luck, Brian. You were my favorite Cardinal, and I don't think I'm alone. I wish you nothing but the best.

# Chris Germer CABOT, ARKANSAS

I became a Cardinal fan because a lot of my family lived in St. Louis and my dad loved the team. My favorite memory is going to my first game. I could not believe how big the field was; I was used to Little League fields. My favorite player would have to be Ozzie Smith. He was a great player and a great person. He stuck with the team when they were really bad and stuck with them when they were good. You don't see a lot of team loyalty today with all of the big paychecks, so that is why he is my favorite.

The only Cardinal I have ever met is Bob Gibson. I got his autograph in Omaha, Nebraska, where I used to live and where he also lives. I have the baseball he signed in a glass case, and it is my most prized possession. Bob Gibson is a very nice man, and he still looks like he could throw pitches in a major league game!

# *Peggy Heilig* CHAMPAIGN, ILLINOIS

Some of my fondest memories involve growing up as a Cardinal fan in a small town in southern Illinois. Our radio was almost always set to KMOX, and Jack Buck's voice was as familiar as the voices of people I knew. If one walked outdoors, day or night, during the summer, Jack's voice could be heard coming from radios throughout the neighborhood.

When I was quite young, I was given a book of baseball scorecards, which I filled out while listening. I prefer listening to baseball on the radio. Because of its pace, it is easy to visualize from the play-by-play, and I still listen faithfully. What I find fascinating looking back is how the players and announcers became almost like friends! I had never met these people—many of them I had never even seen—yet I knew them by their first names and wanted them to do well.

My hometown is very, very small, so St. Louis appeared to be an incredibly exciting place. The Cardinals, along with Famous-Barr and the Muny Opera, were the most indelible symbols of the city. To this day, I cannot think of St. Louis without immediately thinking of the Cards. I am now in my fifties, so this allegiance has lasted for more than half a century.

I think it's harder to be a fan today, because of the lack of continuity of players. Years ago, fans not only knew the players on their teams, but often knew all of the opposing teams' rosters as well. That's almost impossible now, and I think this change has hurt the game. Nonetheless, baseball will always be my sport, and the Redbirds will always be my team.

# Chad Eichelberger

KINGSTON, TENNESSEE

I have been a Cardinals fan all of my life—it runs in my family. The events I remember most vividly from following my team are the 1987 World Series and the 1996 NLCS. I was there for both and what was most disappointing was losing when we were *so* close. There has only been one World Champion Cardinals team in my lifetime and I was too young to remember it. Something special happened, though, when I went to Game One of the '96 NLCS. Tony La Russa was in front of the dugout. A crowd of Braves fans were gathered around, asking for the baseball he held in his hand. Tony took off his hat and pointed at the St. Louis logo. I took my hat and held it high in the air, and he tossed *me* the baseball. That made my day!

But we lost the game, and as I was walking through the parking lot an Atlanta fan walked up to me and said, "St. Louis who?" From that point on I hated the Braves. I was taunted by pretty much everyone I know because I live in the middle of Braves country. When St. Louis got up three games to one, I thought I was finally going to hear the end of the trash talk. It was one of the best, most exciting feelings I've ever had, but it turned into a huge letdown when the Braves went to the World Series. That just made me want to see St. Louis get there even more, and hopefully I'll see that happen soon.

# Rae Jean Daugherty

MASCOUTAH, ILLINOIS

It was July 4, 1996. My son, Michael, was in a very serious accident and spent two months in Children's Hospital. He was in intensive care for two weeks. During his stay, the social services department suggested then-Cardinal Mark Sweeney visit Michael (Mark loves kids and visited Children's Hospital whenever possible). Michael had a head injury, so his recovery was day by day, and we wanted him to be able to realize who he was meeting when Mark visited. It never came to be, so at the end of August the hospital gave us tickets to a Cardinals game, and we were told we would meet Mark Sweeney in the dugout and be given a small tour.

Michael, my husband and I had a great tour prior to the game. Michael played catch with Mark, and Mark gave him a signed bat and ball. As we were about to go to our seats, Willie McGee came down the hall and Michael was introduced to him. Willie put his arm around Michael, took him into the locker room and showed him around. Michael came out with a soda, a couple of candy bars and a huge smile. Willie also gave Michael a signed bat and ball. Many pictures were taken. The bats and balls hang in my son's room, and they will be treasured forever. Willie and Mark

*Mark Sweeney and Michael on the field for the team's pre-game workout, August 1996.* (Photograph courtesy of Rae Jean Daugherty)

*Michael hangs out with Willie McGee and takes a tour of the Cardinals' clubhouse.* (Photograph courtesy of Rae Jean Daugherty)

are so very special to our family for taking the time to brighten a boy's day, a day that my family holds dear in our hearts.

It's been a little over two years since Michael's accident and he is doing great.

# *Carol Beck*   ST. CHARLES, MISSOURI

### "Mark McGwire's 71st Home Run"

Our family has had so much fun waiting and watching Mark McGwire hit all of those home runs. We were lucky enough to take our three children, ages 10, eight and five, to the last Friday Cardinal home game in 1998, in which McGwire hit home run number 66. The ballpark had a World Series-like atmosphere that day: Everyone was happy and filled with enthusiasm. The following Sunday afternoon was the final regular-season game. We had the game on the radio while we were trying to get some chores finished but would go in to watch the TV when Mac was up to bat. Someone would yell, "McGwire's up!" and the rest of us would run like a herd of impalas being chased by a lion. As McGwire hit number 70, a roar erupted spontaneously from all five of us. We were jumping up and down, hooting and hollering, hugging each other and really enjoying the excitement of the moment.

When the game was over, we went back to our chores of cleaning rooms and finishing homework. Everyone still had the radio tuned in to hear the post-game interview and highlights. We were basking in the joyous occasion but were also a little sad that the season was over. We did not want to let go of the fun baseball had brought into our lives all summer. A few minutes

*Andrew Beck with "Papa" Vernon Schulte at the*
*Cardinals/Cubs game on Labor Day 1998. During the*
*game, Mark McGwire hit home run number 61.*
(Photograph courtesy of Carol Beck)

later, our five-year-old son, Andrew, came darting out of
his room as quickly as he could and ran straight for the
TV room. He was yelling and screaming, "Mom! Dad!
Hurry! McGwire just hit another one! It's number 71!"
Andrew was so excited; he didn't realize the game was
over and what he had heard was the rebroadcast of number 70 on the "Play of the Game." We all had a good
laugh about home run number 71. With big smiles on our
faces, it was the perfect ending to a wonderful summer
filled with family fun, togetherness and excitement!

*Five-year-old first baseman Andrew Beck prepares to field a grounder.* (Photograph courtesy of Carol Beck)

# John W. Maher  ST. PETERS, MISSOURI

The baseball Cardinals and St. Louis have always been tied together in ways no one outside our city could understand. It's a form of magic I've experienced nowhere else in any sport, and it exists despite whatever the Cardinals' record is in a given year. This is a love affair passed on from generation to generation, and a history of names passed on like an honor roll: Dizzy, Enos, Stan, Cepeda, Shannon, Ozzie, Willie, Clark and Big Mac.

To be raised here was to barbecue to the sounds of Jack Buck, as he painted a picture of the day's game so clear you could see it with both eyes closed. It was going to Sportsman's Park as a Cub Scout to see Stan Musial play. It was watching Lou Brock, the original and true "Base Burglar," wearing a Brock-a-brella as he shagged balls in the outfield. It was Bob Gibson's scowl, and knowing he would not allow the beloved Cardinals to lose on that day. It was Willie and the '82 Series. It's sitting in Big Mac Land with the kids and their "Straight A" tickets. And it's so much more.

For something magical seems to happen to players when they put on the jersey with the birds on the bat. They seem to become once again the children we all are at heart, and their true love of the game returns. They are free to play as they did growing up, before the sport was clouded with canceled series, strikes, agents and walkouts. Here we play baseball as, to quote, "it oughta be." And that tradition exists generation after generation in St. Louis. Two incidents in my life some 20 years apart illustrate this special respect between St. Louis fans and players.

While in high school, my friend Bryce and I were able to secure jobs selling souvenirs at Busch Stadium. Being the mid-'70s, these were not our most impressive years statistically. Gibby was gone. Whitey was years away. There was little to care about if winning was all one sought, as Cincinnati and Pittsburgh ruled the National League. Yet, people still came to town to see the Cardinals. More fans, in fact, than Pittsburgh enjoyed as they won.

Each day after setting up, and while awaiting the opening of the gates, we wandered down to the edge of the field and watched the Cardinal players work out. Being young businessmen, we were quick to retrieve any balls hit into the stands to later sell, never suspecting this would one day be an industry in itself.

During the '70s the Cardinals had a unique personality on their pitching staff. His funny facial hair and incredible act that seemed to break hitters' concentration endeared him to St. Louis at a time when we needed a new hero. Al Hrabosky was St. Louis' "Mad Hungarian," and we loved him.

Though we were just kids, Al was great to us. We got to see him before the games, before he put on the angry stare he used on hitters. And we knew: No player ever enjoyed playing ball more than Al did back then. Two days in a row, as he sat along the wall watching others throw in the Cardinals' bullpen, we

ran up to Al and asked him to sign the balls we had retrieved from the stands. He never refused as stars so
often do today.

Al asked us what we were doing with the balls he
signed. We told him we sold them at our stand for big
bucks to out-of-towners seeking the great souvenir to
take home and show their friends. After laughing for a
moment, he signed our baseballs, then took one of the
finest balls and asked a favor in return. This one, he
told us, was to go for free to a youngster who appeared to be a great fan but didn't have any money.
And he trusted us at our word it would be done as he
had asked.

That day a young boy about seven years old lin-
gered at our stand several times. It wasn't hard to see
that he didn't have money enough for even a pencil
with the Cardinal emblem. In our rush to sell, we
dropped a 10-dollar bill, which he saw and retrieved.
He gave us our money back when we didn't even know
it had fallen. To him went the magical ball, as Al had
asked. The boy's father came back with him a few minutes later to return the ball, thinking it had been ob-
tained in some wrong manner or was a mistake. But,
after we explained the story, I thought for a moment I
saw tears in that dad's eyes as he and his son walked
off hand in hand, the child's grin bigger than the
Cheshire Cat's. I think often of that ball sitting somewhere and that boy showing it to the world—a gift to
him, from the Mad Hungarian.

Two decades later my 14-year-old daughter stood
in a large crowd along the dugout on the first-base
side with thousands of others, awaiting the first St.

Louis appearance of the newest Cardinal, a guy named Mark McGwire. The rush was incredible as Big Mac appeared, and as this giant of a man with the big heart always does, he tried hard to sign everything held out to him. He must have signed his autograph a hundred times.

Finally, only feet away, he reached the spot where my daughter held out her new glove. As his fingers held the glove, tragedy struck: Big Mac was called away for his turn in the batting cage. He handed back her glove and went on to where the media awaited to watch his batting practice. Her face fell, and I thought her heart would break. To be so close.

But, I wasn't alone in what I saw. Before she could move from the spot she was pinned into by the crowd, a young Cardinal covered a distance of about 20 feet. He reached into the crowd, took her glove and signed it carefully across the side, even though by doing so he subjected himself to many minutes of signing autographs when he seemed to have much to do in preparation for the game.

From that day on John Mabry became my daughter's hero, and my newest hero in a long list. If John is hurt, she is sad. If John is hitting well, she is happy. And that John Mabry–signed glove sits in honor with our collectibles. For it represents all that is good in the men who wear the St. Louis logo.

Someday, my daughter will tell this story to her kids, and they will look at the glove in awe. And, as is St. Louis tradition, another generation will hear the roll call. They will hear about the men who wore the uniform and played hard and never forgot the people who loved them, the fans who supported them when they were down and cheered them in victory. The game will live on in St. Louis. And that's baseball like it oughta be.